A Journey of Thoughts

Uncommon thinking to free your
heart and uplift your soul

Merriene Scott
A JOURNAL

First Published in 2024 by Soul Grace Publishing

This book is copyright and all rights are reserved. No part of this publication may be reproduced, stored in a retrieval system or transmitted in any form or by any means - electronic, mechanical, photocopying or otherwise - without the prior permission of the publisher. No responsibility can be accepted by the author or publisher of this book for any action taken by any person or organisation relating to any material contained herein.

The author of this book does not dispense medical or psychological advice nor prescribe the use of any technique as a form of treatment for physical, psychological, emotional or medical issues without the advice of a physician, either directly or indirectly. The intent of the author is only to offer information of a general nature to help you in your quest for emotional and spiritual well-being. In the event you use any of the information in this book for yourself, the author and the publisher assume no responsibility for your actions.

The moral right of the author has been asserted.

Copyright © 2024 Merriene Scott. All rights reserved.

National Library of Australia Cataloguing-in-Publication data:

ISBN-13: (paperback edition) 978-0-9751058-3-2
ISBN-13: (e book) 978-0-9751058-4-9

Cover photo of North Cottesloe beach, Perth, Western Australia by Merriene Scott

Other books by the same author:

Scott, Merriene. *"The World Beyond Today,"* WA, Australia. 2001
Scott, Merriene. *"Adventure into Transformation,"* WA, Australia. 2003
Scott, Merriene. *"Ancient Memories, New Beginnings,"* WA, Australia 2004

Dedication

*This book is dedicated to all
seeking to evolve
into a higher state of consciousness.*

"The Earth is on a course that will take it into the next millennium with splendour and pain.
The pain will be the falling away of old structures and institutions that have served the human of the past.
The splendour will be hailed by the Fifth Dimensional Human who will see the manifestation of all things become possible within a twinkling of an eye.
While chaos appears to be surrounding you in this moment of time, rest assured that out of all the motion and unfamiliarity rests the pattern of the blueprint of the Divine."
Ascended Master El Morya 1992

"It's only a thought, and a thought can be changed."
Louise Hay

ACKNOWLEDGEMENTS

Life has a way of producing the right people at the perfect time. Divine synchronicity.

My loving gratitude to my good friends Merriel Perrin and Jenny Jones, both Perth residents, for early reading of this manuscript, and advice and support to continue with confidence.

One of my precious earth angels Marianne Burns (another Perth resident) has, with her incredible generosity, been with me every step of the way. Her exceptional eye for detail and correctness has improved the flow of the written words. My abundant gratitude and love.

My wise friend Peter Krusi who divides his time between Zurich, Switzerland and a fabulous farm at Quairading, Western Australia has provided wonderful feedback, firstly with all my newsletters I have sent to him over the years and then encouraging me to convert them into a book.

Another marvellous earth angel is my editor Jennifer Marr, who with her gentle kindness, thoroughness and continual belief in my writing has journeyed with me to create this production of thoughts. It has been a loving, delightful sharing time. My heartfelt gratitude.

Many family members and friends have in their own unique way respected and supported me during the writing process. Thank you.

And thank you dear reader for selecting this book.

CONTENTS

Foreword xiii
Introduction xv

1	Waking Up	1
2	Awakening	3
3	Shining Your Brilliance	6
4	Time of Celebration	9
5	Our Temple	11
6	Lightening Up	13
7	New Year's Gifts	16
8	The Unseen Loving World	18
9	Synchronicity	20
10	Keys	23
11	The Bridge	25
12	Belonging, Bringing, Becoming, Being	27
13	Signs and Patterns	29
14	The Butterfly	32
15	Sovereign Self	35
16	Gifts to Share	37
17	Change	40
18	The Stage is Planet Earth	42
19	Fear Versus Love	44

20	Every Upset is a Set-Up	46
21	Intention	48
22	Honouring the Past	51
23	Embracing Death	53
24	Meditation	55
25	Gratitude	58
26	The Courage to Endure	60
27	Passion	63
28	Creating Miracles	65
29	Defiant or Compliant	67
30	Seeking Truth	70
31	Find Your Purpose	72
32	Changing Frequencies	74
33	Grit	77
34	Breathing	79
35	Negatives into Positives	81
36	Climate Change	83
37	A Grand Design	85
38	Wisdom and Grace	87
39	Sacred Geometry	89
40	Ancestral Lineage	91
41	The Beach	94
42	Do and Be Your Best	96
43	An Attitude of Love	98
44	Multidimensional	100
45	Unconquerable	103
46	The Gift of Grief	105

47	Desirable Beliefs	107
48	A Simple Life	109
49	Forgiveness	111
50	Willingness	113
51	Animal Love	115
52	Rescuing Ladybugs	118
53	Wonder of Nature	120
54	Rowing Your Own Boat	122
55	Being Human	125
56	Recognition	127
57	Magic Happens	129
58	Reflections	131
59	Moral Compass	133
60	We Are What We Think	135
61	Changing Paradigms	137
62	We Are Nature	139
63	Purity and Love	141
64	Decluttering the Brain	142
65	A Deeper Declutter	144
66	Merriment	146
67	The New Children	148
68	Wise Choices	150
69	Your Calling	153
70	Uniting	155
71	The Soul's Music	157
72	Good Vibrations	159
73	Know Thyself	161

74	Angels	163
75	Riding the Waves	165
76	Endings and Beginnings	167
77	Seasons	170
78	Questions	172
79	The High Road	174
80	The Energy of Love and Peace	176

Appendix 179
End Notes 185
Recommended Reading 187
Feedback from Readers and Clients 189
About the Author 193

FOREWORD

We are the collective of wisdom from a high source of energy, and we will call on the most divine and wise energy of the Christ, Sananda (Jesus), to speak with you now.

A Message of Love

"My divine and beautiful friend(s). I am with you with much love and honour.

We are all working together to bring about a collective knowing of the way to move forward in this world of yours, with all the disparate energies now at play. We have need to calm the violent forces and bring about harmony and balance once again.

It is now the opportunity to right the untruths that have been presented by the power players during the centuries. I am the energy of *love,* and this is what we need to bring forth in abundance.

Hate and fear have no place any longer, and it is in the panic of the dark forces that the atrocities are continuing.

Education is the only way to change the thinking and action of humanity. The new generation knows this and as they come into leadership positions, the dynamics will finally change, and the new world will become one of greater peace.

Remember the message is always one of loving kindness, compassion and understanding between all humankind."

Sananda – with great love
(Channelled through Merriene.)

INTRODUCTION

It is with great pleasure I share with you my thoughts, feelings, experiences and knowing through the following pages.

This book is based on my monthly newsletters from the past few years. Some of you may have read parts of this through those newsletters, while others may be new to my work. Either way, I welcome you to enjoy the messages within these pages.

Much of the last twenty years or so has been an incredible journey of *becoming*. Along the way, I have assisted many beautiful clients to awaken to, or confirm, they are divine consciousness here in human form. Also, to understand they are experiencing a life in which to accomplish a mission and contract they set in place before they were born. There have been many transformations and manifestations for them.

My life work has been a privilege and responsibility. My gift as a psychographic medium has allowed me to be a conduit for clients to connect - through automatic writing - with their spirit guides, angels, higher self and loved ones who have returned to the spirit world.

The feedback from my clients confirms this connection and so many appreciate having in writing the exact dialogue from their spiritual messengers. In fact, a great number have said that the writing on the paper has a special energy that gives them reassurance and confidence to move forward in life, even many years after their sessions.

Know each of us matters in our own unique way, and all that matters is *love*.

The three-dimensional world can be challenging and perplexing. However, as you awaken and expand your awareness into the multidimensional, metaphysical existence, of which we are all a part, you will find the knowing of who you truly are will bring you wisdom and peace.

Enjoy the read.
Merriene

ONE

Waking Up

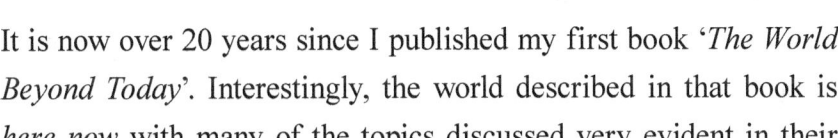

It is now over 20 years since I published my first book *'The World Beyond Today'*. Interestingly, the world described in that book is *here now* with many of the topics discussed very evident in their happening today.

A statement I read recently says:

> *"We have wreaked havoc on nature, and now nature is wreaking havoc on us!"*

… as witnessed in the extremes of weather, rising sea levels, biological illnesses (Covid-19), and the hopelessness and lack of purpose of many people.

There is *information overload, stimulation overload* and *pollution* (toxins - electro- magnetic, chemical etc*) overload.* Many people are still 'asleep' and have not awakened to the sacredness of our home, planet Earth and through greed or thoughtlessness have not considered how fragile conditions are becoming. We need to restore harmony and balance.

Our bodies and environment are being bombarded continuously with poisons which are damaging our immune systems; hence so much illness.

The Covid-19 pandemic is perhaps a message to humanity to find a kinder, purer, simpler way to live. To value what we have and remember that we are wise and wonderful souls here to lift consciousness to a higher level. We are currently in a paradigm shift, experiencing a reset for humanity as we begin a new era of existence.

Many young people are awake and have great clarity about climate change and what needs to be done. They value the Earth as their home, much more than many of the older generations who have taken this planet for granted.

It's time to ask ourselves, "What can we do to bring about balance and harmony once again?" It's important to not only ask this question, but to find answers and act upon them.

We need to be discerning with our actions in this new reality. As a groundswell of meaningful change *is* now beginning to happen. So have trust and take heart.

No matter what happens keep shining your beautiful light.

TWO

Awakening

I consciously began my communication with spirit through automatic writing in 1995. I say 'consciously' as we are all constantly connected with spirit (God, Prime Source, our guides, angels, and higher self) whether we are aware of it or not. Most young children have a strong knowing of their great bond with this dimension and this becomes suppressed when lack of encouragement and confirmation from family and peer groups does not support this bond as they grow.

My journey of discovery and exploration since this conduit was opened (or reopened) has been magical, challenging, and uncompromising for me. Once I had the realisation of this sacred connection we have with the wisdom of Universal Consciousness, my perception of reality expanded with great wonder and awe.

We are never alone and all our experiences, whether joyful or tragic, are to assist us to evolve into the wisest and grandest souls we can be and therefore contribute to the collective consciousness of existence.

So, remember, whatever your situation in life, you are a soul of great courage playing a valuable role for the greater good.

The moment we realise we have the ability, as we all have, to communicate and receive assistance from spirit and our higher self, our life becomes more purposeful, and meaningful. It also becomes sacred. From this standpoint, we experience greater peace and confidence knowing we have a reason for being, and that we are loved and cared about from a higher plane of being.

Since I began to communicate and tune-in for people, becoming a conduit for well over a thousand clients, magic happenings have occurred. For as they trusted the process and gave themselves permission to access this higher wisdom, they were able to make wiser choices in life and change their perspectives on their dilemmas.

It has been so rewarding for me to receive feedback on some of the wonderful shifts and changes that have come about very quickly for them after a session with me.

We are all much more than the person we think we are in a human body. In consciously connecting with our greater selves and the higher universal wisdom we allow this magic to happen.

So, take the time to talk with your spiritual friends (guides and angels) as well as your higher self. It may be through meditation, contemplation, hearing, seeing, knowing or writing. My way is through writing (my human design!).

Enjoy a magical and comforting time with them. Understand we are eternal beings, here for an adventure and new experiences. Relax and trust all is as it needs to be.

I began my journey with automatic writing after I was told, by a wonderful spiritual counsellor, this would be the best way for me to connect with spirit. I describe how I began this in my first book *'The World Beyond Today'*.

"Automatic writing (or intuitive writing) can be described as accessing the inner voice giving 'spirit' the opportunity to communicate through the writer, who is willing to be a conduit for this process.

Some will say this is having a direct link with God and your higher self.

Automatic writing for clients involves the client asking 'spirit' the questions that are important to them, via the counsellor/writer, who will receive some gentle messages and suggestions for this client through automatic writing. Ultimately it can assist them to find their own answers.

The writing is then given to the client to keep, and in the re-reading further insights and understanding can be gained."

I have clients who have returned to see me many years later (sometimes up to 15-17 years) after rediscovering an earlier writing and finding how useful it had been – and still is!

Experiment and reach out through writing if this appeals to you after relaxing, meditating for a moment or two, and perhaps then using your less dominant hand to write. You may find a wonderful connection happens.

THREE

Shining Your Brilliance

Message from Spirit

"We are with you with love. Love is powerful and as you love yourselves you have greater capacity to love others.

This is the failing in the world of yours as most people seem to be consumed by hate, anger and/or a sense of worthlessness. This is perpetuated with each generation and learnt behaviour. The capacity to hate breeds humans who are not able to be full of love, generosity and compassion.

With the state of the planet now, with the many wars, the pollution of the environment and the desire of many people to have gratification at any cost, the spirit of them is lost and confused.

It is the understanding that you are a beautiful spirit having an experience as a human that is not remembered by the many. So, for those of you who do remember it is most important for you to be a shining light in a dark world.

You are the ones who will show the way for those who are lost and confused. It is not an easy path; however, you know this is what you have chosen to do this lifetime. So, stay strong and brilliant in your knowing.

Blessings from the messengers from Illanitis"

(When I began writing my earlier books many years ago, I was told it was the messengers from Illanitis who were assisting. (I'll an(d) it is). I now know it means 'I will, and it is'. It is the truth within us all, speaking to us.)

The above message is a reminder to us all to live with our highest truth and moral compass.

Many events occurring in the world continue to bring attention to the lack of morality, compassion and empathy, as well as the greed and disharmony present at this time.

Here in Australia recently, the focus was on a visit to the Vatican in Rome by the survivors of historical childhood abuse. They were able to be present as evidence was given, via computer link, at a court hearing into past abuse committed by Catholic priests in Australia. These survivors were and still are looking for answers and accountability for all they suffered – and are still suffering to this day.

While at a Writers Conference in Maui, Hawaii in 2002 I met up with a writer from Washington State, USA, who as a very young girl had lived in a Catholic-run Magdalene laundry in Ireland. She had suffered from abuse and was subjected to work in unpaid labour for many years until she managed to break free. I read her story, visiting her in America later and know these former residents eventually received compensation, but only when many of them, such as my friend, were courageous enough to speak out.

Interestingly, the movie *'Spotlight'*, released around the same time, was announced as a winner of an Academy Award. Its subject matter was focussed on this very topic, that of child abuse within the Catholic Church in Boston in the USA.

Remember: -

*"We are with you with love. Love is powerful
and as you love yourselves
you have greater capacity to love others."*

FOUR

Time of Celebration

The festive season of Christmas and New Year is for many a traditional time of great celebration. But for many others it is a time of emotional upheaval and reflection of their situation in life, which may be one of loneliness and hopelessness. Many fortunate people do enjoy the season, sharing with family and friends the joy of coming together with the rituals of this time. Either way, it is a time of the year which usually brings about truth of feeling during these annual rituals, gift buying and feasting for some, or lack of, for others.

Yet, the season of Christmas was at one time in the Northern Hemisphere a celebration of the passing of the shortest day of the year and the welcome of warmer days to come. It was chosen by early Christian leaders to celebrate the birth of Jesus on that day even though it may not have occurred on the 25th of December.

I interpret *Christ–mas* as a time for each of us to celebrate our *Christ–al* within; the beautiful inner Crystal. This is our pure sacred self, that part of us divinely connected to God, Prime Source, the Universal Consciousness or whatever you consider it to be. Hopefully it is shared with authentic love, thoughtfulness, kindness and generosity remembering this pure crystal within every one of us.

We do not need to have elaborate and exhausting rituals for this. Acts of kindness and thoughtfulness are the best part of the spirit of Christmas – and we are encouraged to do so all through the year. Why only at Christmas?

We all have different interpretations and perceptions of the significance of Christmas with many having other beliefs and others being in a place of trauma, loss and sadness. If possible, reach out to those in need and show them their life is worth living. If you are on your own at that time, celebrate your own divine self.

So, whatever your circumstances, remember to have mindful celebrations of both yours and others' magnificence as courageous and perfect souls here on the planet experiencing all we have chosen this lifetime.

May we shine our lights brightly, be strong, pure of intention and kind to ourselves and others. Know you do matter.

FIVE

Our Temple

Do you have a loving relationship with your body?

I hope so.

It is your 'temple'.

It is your vehicle/car/ka to house your soul/spirit/personality for each lifetime.

It is your Earth Suit (explains Gary Zukav in his book *'Soul Stories'*) for the experiences we then have.[1]

The more loving, reverent and appreciative we are of it the more lovingly it will serve us.

Do you remember *Masaru Emoto* and his experiments with frozen crystals of water?[2] He took photos of these frozen crystals after he had either spoken to the water with love or with a harshness. The resulting photos showed great beauty in the lovingly spoken to samples and great distortion in those of the harshly spoken to water.

Importantly, our bodies are made up of a high percentage of water. Treat it well and only put into it the very purest of ingredients that enhance and nurture your cells to do the work they are designed to do. The key is to think of it with great respect.

There is always a magnificent symphony in production, creating harmony and balance. Our immune system will serve us well if we honour it and do not consume poisons such as drugs, alcohol or synthetic chemicals. There are already too many poisons in our environment that the body needs to deal with. The result of toxic substances in our body is disharmony and dis-ease, as the body protests and reacts to a now discordant symphony. In this way, we make our internal environment as polluted as our external environment. Choose wisely.

As we step into each New Year and the continuing challenges we face, thinking, feeling and acting positively with love, will keep us uplifted and in our sovereignty. Our brilliant light will be noticed, assisting many in need to enhance their own light.

SIX

Lightening Up

In my earlier books I discussed letting go of fears and expectations so we can move forward to new levels of consciousness. As well as these vital changes it is essential also to let go of things – material possessions - that no longer give us joy or have purpose in our lives.

A New Year resolution for me was a cleaning out of the stuff I have accumulated over many years. I still have a long way to go, and have wondered, "Why do I wait for the New Year?"

January began with the arrival of my son Digby and his lovely family from their home in New Zealand for a holiday. We discussed our plans for the year ahead and I stated my aim to thoroughly clear out my rooms of unnecessary clutter. I was made more acutely aware of this when preparing for the arrival of these five extra family members in my home.

A few days later Digby gifted me a book *'The Life-Changing Magic of Tidying'* by Marie Kondo.[3] It was of great assistance to help discard what does not bring joy or is no longer necessary. Many of you may have also read it by now.

I gave away many clothes, a child's travel cot that had not been used for about eight years (and is now being well used by a good friend when her grandchild stays with her) and discarded sample toiletries etc. An old laptop computer and broken cameras have gone to an electronic recycling depot; I felt I was just beginning!

In this clearing out I became clearer in my thinking, feeling, and planning for the year ahead, despite extremely hot weather in Perth at that time. It helped me to see the next level needing to be cleaned out. These included files of old courses I had attended and books I had read along the way to help me discover more about the meaning of life. They were very important and valuable at the time, and I am extremely grateful for having had access to them. I see them as material for primary/high school learning and now I am enjoying university learning. Perhaps it is the same material but at a more complex or deeper level.

So, why keep what has served me well but is no longer necessary? I suggest, if you are in need, begin the task of clearing and discarding all that is no longer useful or joyful in your life and this applies not only to possessions but people, habits, fears and expectations.

It will help to change the energy of your surroundings, circumstances and personal being to that of purity, clarity and readiness for magic to arrive. You are inviting it in by your actions and intentions. Enjoy!

Sometime later…time has gone on and I am still decluttering my home. It is a slow process. I am attempting to do a little every day, even if it is one drawer or shelf. At times I have placed quite a few items on the road verge when we have a roadside council pickup of junk. It is helping me feel lighter and clearer in my thinking. Little by little is better than nothing at all.

I have also been decluttering the paperwork in my study. My focus on this comes and goes, and I know I need to be ruthless. There is so much of interest to revisit as I go through the files. As I sort, I ask myself, "How long since I opened this file? Do I really need to keep this just to jog my memory that I did go to that wonderful workshop? Will it be useful to me in the future?"

My mind plays tricks. I have decided to throw away what is obviously irrelevant and put the rest into a next round pile to look at again later. It takes the pressure off and at least I am slowly whittling away the bulk of the paper.

I came across a business card holder full of business cards, mainly from 10-15 years ago, from many inspiring and successful people. The years have gone on and I realise most of us have moved on in our lives and careers. They were precious learning and sharing years and yet we are all constantly evolving. It is necessary to let go of where we may have been at each part of our life and embrace this now moment. If I am meant to synchronise with any of these lovely people again it will happen without me having to hold on to their, perhaps, outdated business cards. So, into the recycling bin they have gone.

When it is winter, I prune my one beautiful white rose bush (as well as other plants in need) in readiness for the arrival of the new growth in spring. This is a reminder for us all to prune the old from our lives ready for new beginnings.

Being a soul in a physical body requires for us to deal with this physical reality – including possessions. It is not always easy. How are you going with this?

We are entitled to our comforts and things that give us joy. However, to me, having clutter does not give me joy or allow me serenity or clarity. It is still a work in progress. My dear friends say, "I have a very calming, joyful and clutter free home," and yet I know the cupboards are still full of now unnecessary things.

At least change is happening. The energy is shifting – I am clearing the past to enjoy the present more.

SEVEN

New Year's Gifts

One New Year began with the arrival of a wonderful and gifted house guest, a wise shaman, who had travelled from her home in Amsterdam to my home in Perth, Australia.

During her ten days' stay we shared endless spiritual truths and ideas, along with delightful visits to my local beach at North Cottesloe. Here we swam in the clear and beautiful water alongside the white sandy beach. It was the height of summer so there were many hot days and balmy nights. Watching glorious sunsets warmed our hearts.

As it was with her visit, sometimes by pausing, having fun and fully appreciating nature, profound wisdom and deep insight is gained without effort. We stayed in a sacred space intent on the beauty and magic of existence, shining our light of being in order to be of assistance to those around us. As a result, synchronistic happenings and meetings occurred as if by magic!

My message to you now - as each New Year commences - is to be true to you, have independent thought, immerse yourself in the beauty of nature, be kind to yourself and others, be the director of your own path in life and remember there is less need to be heard. You exist, and you don't need other people's acceptance to prove it.

Each New Year is ours to create and fulfil our highest potential. Can you embrace the new and let go of the old hurts and worries? Forgiving yourself of your past actions, those that may have been thoughtless and uncaring, is a powerful and positive action to take.

Embrace the clean slate forging new pathways and opportunities. Know that time is a three-dimensional interpretation. All is really happening in the now. There is no past or future.

So, create a better now by thinking and feeling with an expression of joy and love in all you are doing and being.

EIGHT

The Unseen Loving World

Having resumed a neglected habit of snorkelling over the reef at the fringe of my lovely local beach I am reminded of the wonderful unseen life below the waves. Especially when many of us just gaze at the surface of the water without considering the underwater world which awaits. Fish of all shapes, sizes and colours are intriguing to watch and be amongst, living their lives as best they know how.

My usual habit is to swim across the natural pool from reef to reef and back again, with not much thought being given to what lies beneath, not even sharks. It is staggeringly beautiful in this other world. I bemoan the opportunities I have missed in the past to indulge in this liberating and exhilarating experience. Being in the ocean is so therapeutic and viewing this hidden realm takes me to an even more elevated feeling of delight.

As it is a marvellously different world below the surface of the waves, so it is in the air that surrounds us. It too is full of unseen loving energies, unless you are clairvoyant and can see it all, of course. Angels, spirit guides, ascended masters and devas as well as magical symbols, codes and more. They are there for us to acknowledge and communicate with at all times. They visit us in our dreams and encourage us to pay more attention to them so they can give us assistance. Just because most people cannot see them does not mean they are not there.

We are living in a field of vibrational energy that is ever changing and creating forms and potentials of frequencies with which we can connect to have more meaningful lives.

Dive deep into the ocean of life and don't just observe from the surface. Immerse yourself and remember we are all magnificent. We need to play, have fun and live with joy. This will lift the vibration of our planet to a more beautiful frequency.

NINE

Synchronicity

The Perth Writers Festival takes place each year in February. It is a stimulating event looked forward to by lovers of literature, books and writing as well as many of us who reside in this area.

This year was no exception. I went along on the first day with no particular plans on which lectures I'd attend, apart from one at the beginning of the day given by Barbara Arrowsmith-Young. An inspiring author and educator, Barbara shared her journey from a childhood of learning difficulties, to discovering a way to overcome them through what is now known as neuroplasticity. Her book is *'The Woman who Changed her Brain'*.[4]

After this wonderful lecture I decided to relax, go with the flow, get a coffee and perhaps go to the bookshop before attending another talk in two hours' time. Yet, the Universe had other plans for me! With hot coffee in hand, I suddenly bumped into a good friend clutching two tickets (one of them spare) to a lecture just about to start on a 'Life of Curiosity.' This session was presented by the international author Alberto Manguel, who had published a book named *'Curiosity'*.[5]

I joined my friend at the talk and then at a delightful *'meet and greet'* with Alberto afterwards, to which she had been invited. I felt as though I was being swept along in a magical tide of wondrous energy. The day was a fabulous experience.

I am sure each of you has had many such experiences; so-called coincidental or synchronistic events. By letting go of control, allowing, being alert and aware, divine energies can come in and assist us to have grand alignments with our purpose for being. The next day I checked my emails and my son Digby's latest blog had arrived. The title of his blog was *'Curiosity'!*

Are you curious? I encourage you to be so and be alert to the synchronistic events in your life and enjoy each day as it unfolds.

Do you like to explore the *why, what, how, when* and *who* of things and events?

I do.

It helps us to make sense of our lives. Most of us want to know our existence is valid.

It helps us to have a greater perspective and understanding.

Without curiosity we can become stuck in our thinking, feeling and habits, holding us back from moving into the multidimensional existence that is available for us.

An illness or accident causes us, if we are curious, to reflect on why this has happened to us. We may say to our self, *"This is interesting – what is the higher or greater reason for this to happen to me?"* There is usually a reason beyond the obvious. Perhaps it occurs so you have an enforced rest giving you valuable space to look at your life and think about new choices available to you?

It also helps us to grow in wisdom when we are in an uncomfortable situation and we need to stretch our thinking and feeling to a new level, adjusting and gaining new tools to cope. Sometimes we look back on a challenging time and see that it was a turning point in our life.

With openness and alertness to curiosity we align and attract to us the synchronistic events that are available to our higher mindset – they will not occur if our hearts and minds are closed.

Being curious to explore the world through travel, testing our ability to adapt to new environments and situations as well as gaining knowledge through reading and watching documentaries all contributes to a broader and appreciative insight into the diversity of existence.

Stretch your capabilities, move out of your comfort zone, and expand your curiosity. Fascinating synchronicity awaits you if you do.

TEN

Keys

I have always marvelled at how a little key can make such a difference between opening a door - or anything else requiring a key - or not.

This little bit of metal with its particular pattern or code can be so important. Although now there are many other ways to open things such as with electronic controls etc!

Having access to all that is important to us; our homes, cars, safes and so on is part of our way of life. If we don't have the correct key, we do not have access.

We need to reflect on our keys to opening the door to living a meaningful and fulfilling life and gaining a higher level of consciousness.

What are your keys for this?

Some of mine are:

- Living with love, not fear
- Curiosity
- Kindness
- Having purpose
- Recognising the sovereignty of each person
- Reverence for Mother Earth and all animals and plants

- Living in the now
- Letting go of 'stuff', being still and in a state of grace.

I find a great acknowledgement of each other is the saying:

Namaste

> *"I honour the place in you in which the entire universe dwells,*
>
> *I honour the place in you which is of love, of truth, of light and of peace.*
>
> *When you are in that place in you, and I am in that place in me, we are one."*
>
> Sanskrit Blessing

This is the ultimate key to living a good life!

ELEVEN

The Bridge

I feel I am a bridge or link between certain family members, friends and clients who all have different lives. My wise and caring chiropractor suggested it was most important for me to keep my bridge strong through good self-maintenance and loving support from others. Do you have a similar situation?

There are of course other interpretations for being a 'bridge'.

We can travel over our own bridge, within ourselves, from old patterns, routines, and expectations we have always lived by. As we risk to venture forth and step across this bridge to new ways of thinking, feeling, and acting, we open our hearts and embrace this new higher multidimensional frequency that is now here for us.

As aware humans, we can be a bridge to show the way for many people from old paradigms of being and living to the higher frequency of our new reality. Shining our light of knowing and being an example of living with love, not fear, will assist those who are confused and unsure of who they are currently.

Of course, some people are unaware of this bridge to a new way of being. Perhaps now they are waking up to the need to find it?

We can then also reinforce a strong bridge connecting us with the Universal energy of all that is, however you interpret it. In doing so we honour ourselves as the beautiful souls that we all are.

Ask yourself the following:

- *Am I going deeper within myself to reinforce my knowing and light?*
- *Am I letting go of my old 'self' to embrace the new?*
- *Is feeling strange and different, okay? (it is)*
- *Am I strengthening my bridge between my 3D and multidimensional self?*

We cannot remain as we were. Our wisest choice is to accept and honour this new reality. It will be rewarding for those who embrace it. Be gentle on yourself, keep your sense of humour (*impeccable merriment*!) and cross this reassuring bridge to the new with reverence, grace, and ease.

TWELVE

Belonging, Bringing, Becoming, Being

Wow! This shift to our new reality has been happening so fast during the writing of this book– after all the years of prediction and signs of it coming. We are about to go through a portal into a new beginning, if we so choose!

It is a time to go deep into our wise knowing to move though it with strength, positivity and calm.

Recently my dear son *Digby* (www.digbyscott.com) ran a webinar to share strategies on how to best work remotely as leaders. He talked about *Belonging, Bringing, Becoming and Being.*

I will put my slant on these topics from a metaphysical perspective.

Belonging – 'I matter'. We are souls here to contribute to raising the level of consciousness of humanity and each of us matters. At this challenging time of change we need to stay connected with others even if we are in physical isolation. We need to shine our own unique light with an attitude of joy and kindness to ourselves and all others - and demonstrate our high level of wisdom.

Bringing – 'It matters'. It matters that we bring our unique purpose and knowing to the fore in contributing to the enormous change to how life is now and will be in the future. Know it is of value. Know we have chosen to be here at this pivotal moment in the history of humanity.

Becoming – 'I'm growing'. We grow through change. We expand and become more of who we really are. New circumstances give us permission and the opportunity to explore exciting new realities. It is our choice. Our positive attitude and thoughts are critical to how we move through this.

Being – 'I'm great'. We are souls - being human beings - and part of the divine energy of existence. With an attitude of reminding ourselves we are great we are reinforcing that beautiful truth.

>We are all precious and matter.
>It is time to re-evaluate who we are.
>It is time to re-evaluate what matters.
>It is time to re-evaluate how we are being.
>Be joyful, kind, and grateful – being here matters.

THIRTEEN

Signs and Patterns

I have always been interested in signs, patterns, and synchronicities in life. Have you noticed clues and signs in events, places, and names connected to you?

For example: When I was a small girl, I inherited a beautiful doll that had been passed on to my mother when she was a child. I named her *Rosemary*. I now know my shamanic name is *White Rose* and my spiritual name is *Merriene* (I am also called *Merrie*). Rose – Mary (Merrie). Did I know something in my subconscious all those years ago?

When I was around ten years old, I was given a dear little puppy. I named him *Scotty* and years later I married a man with the surname *Scott*.

My son Digby married the wonderful *Kate Blackie*. Years earlier, when my children were young, we had much loved cats called *Katie* and *Blackie*.

Digby and family live in *Wellington,* New Zealand and I live in *Wellington* St, Mosman Park in Perth, Western Australia.

My dear mother was in *Mosman* wing of her nursing home in her final few years of life.

My brother lives in *Fern* Street, and our great grandfather was born in, and lived his early life in *Fearn,* Scotland.

My maiden name is *'McKenzie'*, and our motto is *'Luceo non uro'* meaning *'I shine, not burn'* - a message to be an achiever and not a victim in life.

My married surname *'Scott'* has the motto *'Amo'* meaning *'I love'*. Living with love, not fear, is very important to me, and hopefully to you too.

Surely these have been hints and guidelines to my human design and what my purpose has been this lifetime? I am sure you too have many signs to show you the way forward.

Another wonderful happening for me involves a fabulous painting I have that was given to me early in my teaching career.

I was gifted this landscape, watercolour painting as a farewell present when leaving a school. I had expressed my love of it during a visit to the home of a family whose daughter I was teaching. It was painted by an aboriginal artist named *Revel Cooper,* who in his earlier life (1940s) had been a member of *The Carrolup School of Art.*

This involved a group of Aboriginal children who had been 'stolen' from their families and forcibly detained at the Carrolup Native Settlement in a wheat farming area of Western Australia. These children created strikingly beautiful and accomplished landscapes that expressed their deep connection to country despite having no formal art training and access to only basic art materials. Their work is now recognised worldwide and many of the paintings reside in one of our University Art Galleries (Curtin University) in Perth, Western Australia.

I have loved my painting for many, many years and hung it prominently in every one of my homes. It was only when, after many years, I opened to my spiritual understanding, I recognised the hidden signs and figures within the painting. They had been there all along, but I was not capable or ready earlier to connect with them. They are codes to assist me during this life journey and are of deep spiritual significance.

Is it prescience; having prior knowledge of events before they take place? Are they clues to our destiny? No matter what, listen to your inner knowing as you make your choices and be alert to the amazing so-called coincidences in your life. Know we are part of a divine plan.

Which signs can your see in your life right now?

FOURTEEN

The Butterfly

*"Just when the caterpillar thought the world
was over it became a butterfly."*

I recently came across this English proverb on a gift card when I was browsing for a birthday card for my wonderful granddaughter. I took extra interest in this wise saying as only a few evenings earlier I had watched a brilliant documentary on TV featuring *Sir David Attenborough* about the beauty of flying.

David explained about the wonder and magical flying abilities of animals and insects. Painted Lady butterflies fly on their flight paths three thousand miles to West Africa from Europe with an inbuilt compass and directed by the sun, in just a few days.

I feel there is a message for all of us in this proverb.

Being the 'caterpillar' is necessary preparation for us to become our own unique 'butterfly'. We all have an inbuilt compass to transform ourselves and fulfil our highest potential. We need to have belief in ourselves and trust we are capable of magnificent achievements.

However, we do not need to remain as a 'caterpillar'. Change happens when we are living the best we can be at every moment and have powerful belief in our ultimate destiny, which is to be a 'butterfly'.

Perhaps, like me, you can change your name to reflect your new persona in the beautiful butterfly state of being, change your environment or even just your habits and way of thinking.

Caterpillars finally become butterflies after spending time in their cocoons. For us this can be seen as 'the dark night of the soul'. They emerge triumphantly from their cocoon to be the best they can be. Does the caterpillar know it is to become a butterfly? Does it know the transformation it needs to go through? How does it know it needs to create a cocoon in which it will go through the process to transform?

We can ask these questions of ourselves at this time of 'metamorphosis.' Perhaps many of you are aware of the need to go through this uncomfortable and challenging time for much needed change to happen? Perhaps you are prepared to be in a cocoon so you can emerge as the new, different, and more brilliant and vital you?

Are you aware, awake, allowing and accepting and letting go of the 'old caterpillar' you? If so, you will be able to 'fly' and move quickly to where you can be of service. You can establish a new 'persona' without limits. You will have shed your old 'body' image and habits and can now shine brightly.

The stressful merry-go-round of living for many - business, politics, and social events etc - hopefully will be stripped back to be more genuine and meaningful.

Many people, sadly, will not come out well on the other side of this testing time as they go through this experience with fear and negativity and will not allow the opportunity for transformation.

Look forward with optimism, knowing we can all have a purer, simpler, and more authentic way of living with greater gratitude and respect for each other and the world we live in once this time of great change is over.

Embrace this new you, be kind to yourself and always have love in your heart.

FIFTEEN

Sovereign Self

Do you see your future? Being empowered, one with more clarity of knowing, living more simply, having more loving connections, less stress, more delight, and autonomy.

These past few years have been incredibly strange and devastating for many. The changing paradigms of reality are happening, due to the Covid-19 virus.

Note: *Corona* = crown (sovereign). This is our wake- up call. We have traded individual truth for conformity.

An interesting book I have recently read is *'Personal Sovereignty'* by Adrian Emery.[6] He explains there is an urgent need for all of us to claim our personal sovereignty and power. We need to decide by and for ourselves to be responsible for ourselves.

It is up to each one of us to uphold the vibration of light and always have an attitude of love and not fear. Following are a few suggestions for you to adhere to:

- *Question all you are asked to conform to and only do what feels right for you.*
- *Use common sense, be responsible and remember to express your individuality and creativity.*

- *Do not be suppressed.*
- *Be detached from the dilemma.*
- *Do not surrender to mass thinking and information.*
- *Begin to investigate and explore new ideas and ways of becoming and doing.*
- *Be an independent thinker.*
- *Be an influencer to lovingly inspire and inform those looking for answers.*
- *Your potential is to be free and a beautiful, powerful energy to help make a difference for a much better and balanced world in which to live.*

Shine your light and be at peace.

SIXTEEN

Gifts to Share

I have been reflecting on the uniqueness of each one of us and thinking of my two independent, creative adult sons and how different and wonderfully individual they are. I am blessed.

My younger son Jamie has, amongst many, a gift for capturing visual wonder and the magnificence of nature. He is a Big Wave surfing photographer based in Margaret River, Western Australia (www.jamiescottimages.com) and has a passion for all water activities and action.

My older son Digby, (www.digbyscott.com) based in New Zealand, also has many talents, with photography being one of them. He is also a gifted wordsmith and executive leadership coach inspiring many to reach their maximum potential and be effective leaders in influential positions.

We are all here to use our gifts no matter what they may be. We have a unique micro biological fingerprint as well as our soul wisdom to fulfil our mission this lifetime.

In my investigations years ago, to discover more about my purpose, I contacted a *'Human Design'* expert. Information is readily available in books and on the internet if you are interested and have not yet explored this.

It has been described as putting astrology, chakras, Kabbalah, quantum physics and genetics in a blender and the result is our individual human design! It is our inner energy field, our energy blueprint.

It clarified for me why I have the gifts I have this lifetime. Why I can so easily have contact with much beyond the physical, bringing through knowledge and information from higher wisdom levels. I can also have conversations with people who are 'dead' and are eager to share their experiences and pass on messages. As I naturally have a high vibration the veil between their world and mine is easily passed through.

One of the aspects of human design I have is to provoke people, cause upheaval and push them (by example) to wake up to the greater truth of our existence. Hopefully I am doing this with my counselling and the books I have written.

By lifting our vibrational frequency and not being in fear (which is what the mainstream media wants us to be so they have control over us) we can tap into this higher consciousness (multidimensionality). It is here we are beyond time and space and the vastness of everything is available to all of us. Remember we are all great.

On my calendar is a quote from Martin Luther King Jr.

> *"If I cannot do great things, I can do small things in a great way."*

On the sea wall in the garden of a house my New Zealand family lived in was a saying:

> *"Be not afraid of greatness."*

And visiting a spell binding immersion experience of Vincent van Gogh's art (he has the same birthday as me) I read this quote:

> *"Great things are done by a series of small things brought together."*

My clients have often asked the question, *"What is my purpose?"*

The replies, through automatic writing by me, have been very individual. One lovely lady was told her best purpose was to sing and give people joy this way. As it turned out, unbeknown to me, she had resumed singing lessons six months earlier after not singing at all for many years.

Those of us with blessed situations can use our unique and individual gifts as best we can to help those in the world who are not so fortunate.

Be the light that you are and shine it brightly, joining up with other beautiful lights, to cast a powerful light into dark places in the world. We can do this with our gifts and compassionate thoughts and prayers if unable to assist in other ways.

SEVENTEEN

Change

The one constant in life is change.

Humanity and the planet are changing. The changing paradigms are painful – a painful rebirth is happening in the world. Do not be in fear. Accept and live with kindness and love to keep light shining.

On a more personal level it is accepted that children grow up, adults grow old and ultimately pass away. Relationships change, circumstances shift, and we need to accept and value what has been, is, and will be. Adapting to the new with a positive and accepting attitude, understanding our greater role in this physical reality, helps us to live in the moment more fully.

Of course, change due to tragedies happening is a tough circumstance to experience.

Through writing with my friends in spirit I have been given a reassuring message for you to assist in your daily life.

"Merriene has asked us here in spirit to write some encouraging words. We are a collective of energy and we bring reassurance for you as a reader that your journey here on the planet is most valuable to the core of your soul group. You may not realise how valuable your interactions; your growing wisdom and your experiences are in giving feedback to us in spirit.

We are the observers of your choices, your reactions, and the beauty of your thoughts. You are never alone, and you can always seek guidance and insight into your dilemmas by connecting with your higher self and own unique guidance.

Remember you create your own reality and, the more loving, and kind you are, the more loving and kinder will be your situations and companions. Trust!"

May you have magical days with a positive and loving attitude in your heart. Embrace all change that happens for you.

EIGHTEEN

The Stage is Planet Earth

"All the world's a stage, and all the men and women merely players. They have their exits and their entrances; and one man in his time plays many parts."
William Shakespeare

It is now a few years since we were informed of Covid-19 arriving in our world. What a ride it has been and continues to be.

The vibrations on the planet have changed, perceptions of reality have changed and people, as part of the human family, have made decisions depending on their level of consciousness. There has been great sadness and angst with many people departing after succumbing to this illness or reacting badly to the injection given to reduce the severity of the virus.

It is pushing many to go deep within themselves to know their soul truth and wisdom when making choices. Always choose the best possible nourishment for your body and the best possible environment you can be in. Do not be in an environment of fear. Keep your immune system strong.

I suggest you ask yourself:

"Do I, with easy acquiescence, let the few, unfairly control the many?"

"Do I research and question everything first, to educate myself and then make my choice?"

"Do I then feel at peace in my heart with what I have decided?"

Freedom is important for all of us. Some people think we are giving it away!

I suggest you avoid the mainstream media information. Sometimes the truth is concealed and you must seek it out. Think for yourself.

Remember you are a beautiful soul (consciousness) having an experience as a human. You are in costume, as 'you', on the stage of life. Your choices give you the experiences you have selected and from which you will gain wisdom, helping you to reach a higher level of consciousness. It is important as you do this to honour and respect, not only yourself, but everyone else in the decisions they make. Even though these may be very different from your own.

It is only a 'play' after all – and the stage we are on is planet Earth. It is such a privilege to be here, as the courageous souls we are, at this time of great change for humanity, to participate in the current upheaval and movement to a new paradigm of being. It is a most uncomfortable time, so keep shining your light, focus on the wondrous beauty and magic around us. Have love and kindness in your vibration always. Have personal responsibility and trust your unique truth.

NINETEEN

Fear Versus Love

During my ongoing sorting and clearing out I have come across a folder containing written messages received from *higher wisdom* during group sessions I held quite a few years ago. The messages are still most appropriate now as we continue to cope with world unrest, violence, and tragedy. Wow, we are continuing to be challenged.

Here are some of those messages after the following question was asked:

> "What is the purpose of the fear and paranoia in people's hearts right now and what can we be doing to clear it?"

Answer:

> "You do know about love, and you know fear is the way of keeping control of the masses. Many beings are wishing to control the masses and to do this they create fear... They know those of you who have great love, and not fear, in your hearts are unable to be under their control.

A JOURNEY OF THOUGHTS

You can assist to educate those in fear to let go of this and understand they are eternal and have nothing to fear.

With love all can be achieved, and beauty will be brought forth again.

Those beings who are keeping the fear in your energy grid are those from the forces of 'dark'. They are your polarity and you have need to reinforce your light and love with all you meet and are with to overcome this unbalanced force.

The force of the 'dark' is in fear itself of losing control and as the lightness grows stronger it (the dark force) is becoming panicky with its actions to keep control. However, as you allow the love of your light to expand, the dark cannot sustain its power.

So, relax and create the beauty of yourselves at all times. With the coming times of loving light and joy we will say this is the last gasp of fear creation!"

We are all being tested in these continuing difficult times on this beautiful planet in our own individual way. Remember (from your higher perspective) you are a wise soul here having an experience in human form and seeing your life journey from this perspective will lessen the fear.

TWENTY

Every Upset is a Set-Up

In 2014 the one hundredth birthday of my amazing mother was celebrated. She was born at the beginning of World War 1 and had lived through the Great Depression, World War 2 and difficult times, experiencing many sad losses and disappointments. However, her outlook had always been positive and her nature appreciative of what life had to offer. She always had a great interest in the achievements of family members, people, and events.

Why is it some people, like my mother, live long, satisfying lives and others have lives cut short by accident or disease?

This is not easy to answer but I consider the length of life will be as long or short as we ourselves script it to be. We are here to have the experiences and tests we have set for ourselves to grow our wisdom and raise our soul consciousness. Sometimes it is to help our loved ones grow in *their* wisdom due to grief from our leaving them and returning to spirit.

There are many tragedies happening across the planet – and always have been. The sudden and sad loss of the plane carrying nearly three hundred beautiful souls in Ukraine a few years ago is only one such example and has brought about many to ask the questions, "Why?" Or "Why that plane, with those precious people?"

A JOURNEY OF THOUGHTS

I was involved (professionally) with the parents of someone who sadly died in this tragedy. There seemed to be so many gifted highly intelligent people, including children, lost who had and may have continued to contribute so valuably to the betterment of humanity.

Perhaps it was part of their script and on a soul level they had volunteered to be part of the airline disaster (as had those who died on 9/11 in 2001 in New York) to bring about greater awareness and change for humanity which unfortunately needs a world tragedy for dynamics to shift.

Having greater awareness that we are a soul here having a human experience may help us to have a wiser perspective of tragedy.

Every *upset* is a *setup!*

TWENTY-ONE

Intention

With the arrival of Autumn rains and cooler days and nights we say goodbye to our lovely long hot summer here in Perth, Western Australia. At this time, I contemplate my constantly changing perceptions about the meaning of everything.

We all have our beliefs, hopes and dreams along with expectations of how life should or could be. With each day these ideas and expectations change depending on our experiences and circumstances.

I attempt to maintain a clear vision and focus of what I know deeply is my own individual reason for being, along with the knowledge we are, by our sheer presence, contributing to a more enlightened collective consciousness of humanity.

By transforming and maintaining ourselves to an energy of loving kindness we are helping to transform the world. By being peaceful in our heart, we are helping to bring light and peace into very dark places. This is a very powerful intention and much needed in this time of continuing upheaval.

Intention is purpose of focus.

Bringing about an intention of being peaceful in our own vibration will radiate a sense of peaceful energy to those with

A JOURNEY OF THOUGHTS

whom we have contact, giving them a feeling of peace and trust. All intention creates our reality, so be clear and pure in what you intend. It will manifest.

So be the best you can be and live with love and peace in your heart.

What is real?

> *"Perhaps, perhaps, perhaps,"* are words sung by the late wonderful singer Doris Day[7] – and what I am now going to say you may think fanciful – and perhaps it is!

Recently I read a great and well researched book, *'Mary Boleyn'* by Alison Weir.[8] She was the sister of *Anne Boleyn*, second wife of *King Henry VIII* of England. Mary and Henry had a brief relationship prior to his marriage with Anne. It seems very likely that a daughter, *Katherine Carey*, born to Mary was the child of King Henry.

Amongst the many descendants of Katherine, and therefore also of Mary and Henry, are *Catherine, now Princess of Wales*, married to Prince William; *Camilla (now Queen)* married to *King Charles*; *Diana, who was Princess of Wales* and mother of William and Harry; the late *Queen Elizabeth II*, and *her mother Elizabeth*.

The above members of the royal family are all genetically linked to Mary and Henry.

In past life/present life possibilities are these ideas, connections and clues:

- *Prince Harry* was *Henry VIII* in that past life.
- His wife *Megan* was *Anne Boleyn*.
- Henry and Anne had a daughter *Elizabeth* who became Queen Elizabeth I of England.

- Harry (real name Henry) and Meghan have a daughter *Lilibet* (*Elizabeth*).
- *Catherine (Princess of Wales)* was *Catherine of Aragon* and the first wife of King Henry VIII. In this life she did have a 'soft spot' for Harry.
- Note the same names, even the name *Megh-an* has a connection to *Anne*.

What is real? How do we know what is true?

It is said there is no linear time, everything is happening now. Perhaps the reality of Tudor times is just a 'slip' of dimensions, and all these members of royalty are playing their many roles, and dramas, simultaneously in a spiral of events.

We all have people in *this* life we have been with in *past* lives.

Fanciful it may be, but perhaps we can expand our awareness to grasp the possibility life is not always as it seems to be.

TWENTY-TWO

Honouring the Past

Travelling to Wellington, New Zealand, has been a lovely annual event for me to spend precious time with my elder son Digby, daughter-in-law Kate and three wonderful and active grandchildren.

One year I also ventured to Albury, in eastern Australia to share valuable time with dear friends I have known since our teenage years.

When with my good friends in Albury, we travelled to Eaglehawk a suburb of Bendigo, which is four hours' drive from Albury. Our visit was to investigate where my paternal great grandfather had established a general store to cater to the needs of the huge numbers of gold miners in the early 1870s. It was a time of gold being discovered in the Bendigo area. My great grandfather, Hugh McKenzie, had arrived with his family from Balintore, (Fearn) in the highlands of Scotland, a few years earlier seeking a better life.

It was for me an emotional moment when we found a very old ruin of a building on what we considered the site of the original store. Whether it was the same building (perhaps improved over time) or not, is not the most important thing for me. It was important I was able to stand on the earth where my courageous forebear had established his first significant business in Australia.

For me, connecting with our genetic ancestors and acknowledging with gratitude our blood line, connecting lovingly with our present family members, and also staying connected with beautiful life-long friends and present friends who honour and understand us, as we do them, is the secret to a happier and more fulfilling life.

Value all that is precious to you.

TWENTY-THREE
Embracing Death

When my dear mother peacefully passed away, she was just five weeks short of her one hundred and third birthday. Her earthly or physical journey this lifetime was complete. She was well pleased with her contribution in creating an inspiring and positive example for how to live to all those who knew and loved her.

Death is only a transition between one reality and another. We are spiritual energy/souls having an experience as a human when we are here in a physical body.

The physical body is our vehicle for our visit here as a human. This enables our spirit/soul to have the experiences in physicality we have chosen to have to gain more wisdom.

There is a sense of wonder about the human body. Each has a unique frequency, a signature of its own. It has great knowledge of each of us to tap into.

We need to honour it and treat it as sacred with nurturing and loving thought, food, exercise and rest.

When we vacate our body and die, it is comforting to have the understanding it is only the physical body, the vehicle, that has departed, and the essence of the person who has gone is still here/there. It makes saying goodbye a little easier.

I have had a few precious conversations with my wonderful, strong mother, and other departed friends and family since they have left, reassuring me of their continuing existence even if it is in a new form!

We are, as I mentioned, eternal, perpetual souls with much to learn on our earthly journey. Each time we are here we remain connected to our soul/higher self, angels and spirit guides, and our departed loved ones if we (and they) so wish.

Do you have this understanding and feel at peace with it?

TWENTY-FOUR

Meditation

Meditation has been known throughout history as the path to spiritual liberation. It is through the activation of our heart centres during meditation that enables our connection with our greater soul or self to strengthen.

It is by stilling the mind that we unveil the beauty of our greater/higher self via the opening of the heart.

The ego/personality rules the mind. Most of us live with our ego/personality being dominant most of the time, allowing very little opportunity for our greater self to bring in our wisdom and intuition.

Through meditation we access this wisdom and gain a sense of clarity and peace. It gives our body a chance to heal, improve our immune system, rebalance and be in greater harmony.

Even a few minutes of meditating a day helps us to live our life in a more empowering and inspiring way. It allows *spirit* to help us where help is needed as we still our mind and open the door, inviting the magical energy to come in.

In 1996 I was fortunate to attend a *Group Primordial Sound Meditation Weekend Workshop* in Perth, with Becky Hansen, a close assistant of Deepak Chopra. We were each given our personal mantra to use during meditation, and I have used it ever since. You can create your own mantra as you listen to your own intuition. It will tell you what is perfect for you. Here is a poem of mine about the heart.

THE BEAUTY OF MY HEART
In the stillness of my mind
Is the beauty of my heart
In the stillness of my mind
I know I am not apart
In the stillness of my mind
Lies the silent preparation
As – in the stillness of my mind
Is the wonder of creation

Aim high and open your hearts wide with the knowledge you create your own reality!

Each time I meditate, even for a few minutes, I have the same routine, as follows:

- I confirm my connection with *the crystalline grid system* with much love and gratitude. My intention here is to acknowledge I am connected to *source* and all that is.
- I ask to bring in *golden liquid light* through my crown chakra to every cell, molecule and atom in my body, and that this beautiful light expands out so others too can enhance their own light.
- I then repeat (silently) my personal mantra – given to me by Becky Hansen all those years ago. It matches my frequency. As I have said, you can find your own mantra through your intuitive knowing.
- I breathe deeply and relax.

Find your own routine that works best for you.

Embracing silence and stillness where we can, will strengthen our divinity. The words *silent* and *listen* are made up of the same letters in different combination. When we are silent in nature and listen to the wonderful rhythms and messages it conveys to us, we can remember our role within it. Listen also to your higher self which will give you clearer messages when you are in your space of stillness/meditation.

Our intention is more important than the details in maintaining our connection to spirit/our light and by doing so routinely we strengthen our hearts as we experience this adventure on planet Earth.

Have a joyful heart.

TWENTY-FIVE
Gratitude

Winter here in the Southern Hemisphere is a time of reflection, reconsideration, recalibration, and regeneration for me. A time of acceptance of all one has experienced in the preceding few months. Of course, in the Northern Hemisphere with the arrival of summer it is a time of taking action and enjoyment of all that is and basking in much needed and important sunshine.

Wherever you are, there is a need for gratitude for everything that is. Everything is perfect in its imperfection and is part of our own unique journey towards higher consciousness.

As is said in my second book, *'Adventure into Transformation'*:

> *"The future is not to be feared but welcomed with joy and excitement for the potential evolutionary growth of humankind. You are at the forefront of this new and amazing transformation of what it is to be human."*

Tragedies such as the huge devastation and loss of life from earthquakes, fires and floods continue to happen as do the moral and ethical challenges facing leaders and organizations. We need to stay centred, balanced and loving whatever our circumstances and grateful for the experiences that help us learn more wisdom.

Focusing on how amazingly wonderful this planet is, we need to view it through a lens of gratitude, joy, and appreciation of the beauty of nature. Knowing that most people have an essence of goodness and act with a purity of loving intention along with hope. This will keep our vibrations high and expand our energy field into a more optimistic field of magical possibility.

Remember we are here to grow in wisdom and raise our level of consciousness through our experiences, choices and attitude.

Enjoy being you in all your magnificence.

TWENTY-SIX

The Courage to Endure

During winter, as I have said, I spend a lot of time just being; going within, surrendering, reflecting, adapting, and trusting. It is a time of refocusing and self-nurturing. There is great joy in appreciating the small things of life – the song of birds, the emerging of hyacinth flowers from bulbs in a pot in my garden with no help from me, vivid double rainbows.

When I wrote this it had been a winter of records, with a great deal of welcome rains here in Perth. There had been many storms, big winds and colder days and nights than usual. In many other parts of the world there have been extremes of weather; floods, droughts, fires and record heat waves. You may have been involved in this somewhere! Have you had need to adapt?

It has been an endurance test (*dictionary meaning (noun) – 'enduring something painful and prolonged'*)[9] for many of us and yet I know what I have just endured is extremely minor compared to the huge suffering of many people. I am most grateful for my fortunate life.

Throughout history many people have had to endure cruelty, horror and hardship. Many pioneers endured with courage and forbearance to pave the way and make life easier for future generations. Much gratitude to them.

An example of incredible endurance by explorers came to attention in March 2022 when the long-lost wreck of the wooden ship *Endurance* was found, after being lost for over a hundred years, where it sank in the Weddell Sea in the Antarctic in 1915. It was crushed by ice and the 28 men on board were stranded for well over a year before Ernest Shackleton, Frank Worsley and four others of the stranded men realised no rescue would happen. So, they courageously set out in a 22-foot boat for South Georgia Island, 800 miles away where there was a whaling station.

After a treacherous journey they finally arrived. It took four months and four attempts to finally rescue the stranded men from their floating ice prison.

All the men survived after having endured freezing weather, limited supplies and very makeshift shelter for so long – and yet they never gave up hope. It has always inspired future generations.

Being the trail blazers many of us 'light workers' are enduring again in many ways to assist humanity to push through into the new frequency of our energy field. The strength of the human spirit prevails. We have a knowing in our soul selves and a memory in our genes to have courage and determination to continue to shine our lights strongly.

These experiences are for 'the getting of wisdom' for our souls.

Love endures, *Hope* endures!

Our personal endurance contributes to the collective endurance. Many people are fragile and can no longer find joy in their circumstances. Remember we are in the discomfort of transformation and lovely, new and beautiful energy *is* coming in on the planet.

Be gentle with yourself and find activities, perhaps simple ones, that give you joy and at the same time can contribute to other people's joy and comfort.

Through all that we endure the flame of *hope* should never go out of our life.

With hope and enduring love there is always a new beginning, no matter what form it takes.

As I wrote this, I noticed outside my study window the emergence of the first tiny green buds on my Chinese Tallow tree. They are having a new beginning despite the battering this lovely deciduous tree has taken during the past stormy few months.

TWENTY-SEVEN

Passion

Many of us have a passion to know more, be more, do more. Being passionate to be more loving, kind, and generous is a wonderful trait to have.

Following our passions helps us to align with our soul's purpose. When we connect with our purpose, we hear and see the signs clearly and act on our reason for being. Our soul knows what our life purpose is and as our personality-self listens to the message of our soul we can, magnificently, fulfil all we are here to do and be. Synchronicity happens more easily when we live our purpose.

When we separate the letters in *passion*, we get pass I on.

We are passing on and imprinting our unique self and journey. We are contributing to the collective, by living our lives as passionately and authentically as we can.

When we have a passion for something and immerse ourselves in it, we usually lose track of time and are one with what we are doing or creating. Artists, writers, singers, designers and creatives across the ages have mentioned this state. I experience this sense of timelessness when I am writing, counselling, and swimming. Think what it is that truly excites you and gives you a sense of joy, fulfillment and being at peace with yourself and the world.

At these times you are truly one with existence.

Many people are passionate about astronomy as they are curious about the universe and stargazing. Recently over forty thousand people all over Australia, star and moon gazed at the same time for ten minutes through binoculars and telescopes to set a new world record for numbers of people simultaneously watching the night sky. This shows real passion.

TWENTY-EIGHT
Creating Miracles

Something truly amazing, wonderful, and miraculous happened for humanity a few years ago.

It was a unifying experience for many people around the world as we witnessed the rescue of twelve young boys and their soccer coach (note: it is the same number as Jesus and his twelve disciples) from deep inside a cave in northern Thailand. The boys had been trapped by rising flood waters for ten days before being found and then rescued. They had no food and the only water available was from little drips on the cave walls. Yet, they had a strong belief and great calmness that they would be rescued and had been taught to meditate by their coach to preserve their energy.

The expertise of the rescuers in bringing them to safety was of the highest order. It seemed as if the whole world, with much prayer and positive thought, were contributing towards the remarkable and magical outcome.

It was a triumph of the human spirit - co-operation between many top cave diving experts from many corners of the world who happened to be available at this time of great need. There was an alignment of favourable energies and I am sure there was supreme co-operation with spirit, from many levels of reality.

Prayer, faith, and optimism set the frequencies for a 'miracle'. Author Barbara Marciniak in her powerful book *'Path of Empowerment'* says:[10]

> *"It is well known that humans are invested with indomitable spirit; that under auspicious circumstances it can be called forth to birth brilliant and remarkable accomplishments."*

It occurred in this rescue mission; an example to humanity of what is possible with co-operation, determination, and loving intention. The outcome is full of joy, unity, and gratitude. We are all part of the oneness of existence.

Be heartened knowing that there are actions of excellence and wonder in this world of ours.

TWENTY-NINE

Defiant or Compliant

Do you tend to be *compliant* or *defiant*? Or sometimes one or the other or both?

Life situations, at times, make us choose to react one way or the other. The implications can deeply affect the consequences.

Recently I observed the reactions of the residents where I live, as the carports at the rear entrances to our townhouses were being replaced with lovely new ones – after drainpipes, soak wells and new paving were put in place. It was a noisy, disruptive time. We had to find new homes for parking our cars for the duration of the upgrades.

Early on, some owners defied the request to park their cars in nearby streets, not realising that the presence of their car near the machinery may have resulted in damage and compromised the work schedule. It was a necessary compliance.

However, being *too compliant*, at times, can make it easier for controlling, manipulative people to rule our life. In these cases, independent, critical and creative thinking by each of us helps us to make wise choices.

Sometimes it is important to be *defiant* when faced with a demand for us to agree to act or decide on an action or issue that our truth knows is not for our highest good or the good of others or the world. Being measured in our reasoning and explanation helps us to be heard.

At times we have rules and standards, whether in the workplace, government or community that are totally outmoded, unreasonable and unworkable due to poor leadership. To change the paradigm, we need to be defiant and speak our truth.

In the years since the beginning of the Covid 19 pandemic I have not spoken expansively of my feelings and thoughts on this. As time goes on more and more is being revealed about the manipulation and coercion during this time. The creation of mandates to drive people to acquiesce to have a jab of an experimental substance that has created 'vaccine injuries' in many of those who agreed to have it, willingly or unwillingly, is indeed a very disturbing outcome.

I ask you: Did you do your research and come to a position of knowledge and understanding before you gave your consent to receive this injection, if indeed you did have it?

There is a need to question everything, to be an independent thinker and at times say, "No." You do not always need to co-operate. We are entitled to make our choice of whether to allow unproven substances into our precious body, and I respect those who have done so.

By all I have researched, the substance in the jab is the very thing that has impacted people's amazing natural immune systems and created havoc with the health of many of those who have been injected. However, the jab was implemented so quickly by bringing people to a state of unfounded fear, pressuring them to comply.

Now the truth is emerging, with many highly respected specialist doctors, successful athletes and researchers courageously speaking out about the danger of the toxins in the product after being muzzled for so long by the mainstream public health authorities and media.

Many others who are greatly concerned are also sharing their experiences. The so-called vaccination has not stopped the spread of Covid, and the so-called protection has been neither safe nor effective.

Many of those who were compliant are now questioning their choice.

Authentic vaccinations are another matter.

Stay strong and have great loving respect for yourself no matter what choices you have made. We are all here to gain wisdom through our experiences.

THIRTY

Seeking Truth

Many of us who are ready, aware and have clear intention are now moving further into being *multidimensional*. As we do this there is some discomfort as we adjust and embrace a further falling away of our old selves.

Listening to our truth and having a direct link with God, prime source and our higher self / soul whatever your belief, is so important now. We all have the ability to connect with this knowing and wisdom that is beyond this physical reality - where we find our divine and authentic self.

As mentioned previously, my ability to reach this wisdom through automatic writing is my *human design* and I am grateful for this gift. I can, as I have said, describe myself as a *'psychographic medium'* and a *'metaphysical philosopher'*.

At these times of connection with the spiritual realm we are in an expanded state of consciousness. It is very comforting, and we realise we are not alone. Our time of being who we are in human form is much appreciated from the higher realms of existence and there in the multidimensional state we gain confirmation of the greater truth of all that is happening.

I encourage you to reach out and explore your ability to connect if you have not done so already. You may be clairvoyant, clairsentient, clairaudient or just *know* things. Through meditation, being in nature, stillness and trusting you will find your vibrations will be perfect for tuning-in to spirit.

These past few years or so with the Covid-19 virus creating a huge reset and paradigm shift for humanity, we need more than ever to stay in our truth. There is so much 'fake' or embellished news and manipulation of our thinking in the media to control the masses.

As you listen only to your *voice of truth* you will have greater clarity, a calmness, and a loving and open heart. You will be a beacon of light for those still in fear as much that has been familiar to them slips away. You can reassure them this reset will assist us to appreciate our lives more fully.

There is no accident we are all here at this time of great change and we are all called to be our authentic and sovereign selves keeping our beautiful lights highly visible.

THIRTY-ONE
Find Your Purpose

Do you know why you exist?

There are many levels of meaning to this question and the answers we may give.

Meditation, contemplation, and deep reflection, as well as reading, may help us find our purpose and to grow in awareness of the wonder and meaning of existence.

As I have said before, we all have a unique journey and purpose. Though collectively we are *all* contributing to raising the level of consciousness for humanity. There are still many people who have not woken up to this awareness.

I encourage you all to find and read books written by intelligent, perceptive, aware authors, watch rational, balanced television documentaries, and do research that will enhance your knowledge and inspire you. Be a worthy contributor to change conditions on this planet for the better.

We all grow in wisdom at our own pace. We can say we all need to go to primary school, then high school and some go on to university. Many find it easier to grasp learning better than others do. Although learning never stops for any of us, we will continue to learn new ideas, concepts, and facts all our lives, mainly through the experiences we have.

Having an inquiring mind helps to speed up the process of gaining higher wisdom. However, there are many people whose souls are still 'young', and they are not ready in this life to understand the deeper meaning of their existence. They will learn in their own time.

All is as it is meant to be. Have love for all - and good reading.

THIRTY-TWO
Changing Frequencies

I am becoming increasingly more uncomfortable with the acceptance by many of the unacceptable levels of violence being portrayed on our television or digital device screens and in the movies promoting the dark side of existence. I see only the ads for these shows as they are inappropriately shown during wonderful art and history programs etc. It is such an insult to the senses.

The anxiety levels of many people, especially our young, are concerning and perhaps it is no wonder, as they are repeatedly being subjected to visions of violence whether they wish to be or not. It's also important to note that domestic violence is not abating.

Also, I am now less accepting of people who are not authentic, not kind and loving and those who create dramas to gain attention. Is it because they feel anxious, unworthy, and confused?

My *vibrational frequency* is changing and becoming more sensitive. I am sure many of you are noticing this about yourself.

This is the time of continuing transformation for many of us – taking us to a higher level of consciousness. At the same time planet Earth is readjusting *its frequency*. As I have mentioned before, the balance and harmony of Earth are fragile – as the serious environmental events continue.

A JOURNEY OF THOUGHTS

Our nature is goodness, and this is being distorted by dark influences. We need to hold on to our joyfulness and sacredness and be the light that we are.

Do not let your light be dimmed.

Our ability to be *telepathic* is becoming easier, as the frequency of our energy changes.

> *"Telepathy is not a voice in the head. Telepathy is the alignment of frequencies between two souls in order to communicate with each other. Telepathy is soul technology."* Anima Mundi

It is tuning in to the correct frequency – changing your radio station until you find the right one for you.

In my first book *'The World Beyond Today'* I wrote:

> "The future will be full of think tanks and thought exchange. You are now in that state a lot of the time with your computers and internet. The telephone also is only thought transference, with the voice as the method of communication for that."

Reading the conscious and unconscious thoughts of others is telepathic in nature.

Have fun with your telepathic skills. The more you practise the easier it will become. Have confidence you have the power to tune in and you can use it for great benefit for humanity. At all times have great respect for people's privacy and use this skill with much reverence.

A few years ago, a few of us from a spiritual group decided to experiment and see if we could heal a 'sick' tree in the garden of one of our group members. We each had a photo of the tree and each morning, in our individual homes, at a set time, we meditated for a few minutes and focused on our tree photo, sending the tree our love. We did this for a week or so.

Within a few weeks the tree was sprouting fresh leaves and on the way to a full recovery. I consider this was *telepathic healing* at its best. Loving thought transfer being received with gratitude by the beautiful tree. So, telepathy can be between all living things – not just humans.

THIRTY-THREE

Grit

Recently the college where, many years ago, my two sons had their high school education, set tasks for students at which they may 'fail' in a week of exercises.

They called it GRIT week – GRIT standing for Growth Resides in Trying - and helped these students to embrace failure and increase resilience.

I call it: *Growth (with awareness) Results in Transformation.*

We've all needed resilience during this past challenging time, and we have all needed GRIT to create positive outcomes in this changing paradigm of our new reality.

In my small back courtyard where I have my clothesline a little spider once resided. Each day, week after week, it spun its web in exactly the same spot. It was a most inappropriate position as, when I placed washing on the line the web got destroyed. (I couldn't avoid it.) On some other days it got blown apart by strong wind or rain. This spider had GRIT - each morning there was a newly created beautiful web in the same position. It did not give up – each day was a new beginning.

We also need to have grit to continue our lives with determination not to give in to the difficulties we may face. Remember we are as the caterpillar in the cocoon and we are changing to become a butterfly – and it is hard-going during this transformation time. Yet, we are nearly there, and will do well to stay strong enough for this metamorphosis to complete.

Open your heart and share your love and kindness with all humanity and especially to those who are important in your life. Celebrate being here – it has taken courage. Keep your vibration high with joy and laughter.

Embrace all you have with gratitude.

THIRTY-FOUR

Breathing

The greatest gift for many people, due to the challenges and hardships many have faced, is we have gained more of our *sovereignty*. We have come back to *us*, who we individually are, what is of value and a remembering we are *consciousness*, not our physical self.

Will we now feel more empowered, no matter what is going on in the world, to stay true to our self and value all we have and are?

It has been an important time for contemplation. It is time to take a deep breath.

Let us focus on breathing more easily now, after a time of breathing 'difficulty' – demonstrated by the smoke and pollution from the many disastrous bushfires around the world, the tragic death of George Floyd who stated, as he lay dying, "I can't breathe," and the death, sadly, of so many from the Covid-19 virus through respiratory failure or due to vaccination injury.

Plants and animals have also suffered hugely through this changing environment and circumstances.

In this new, very different paradigm of existence:

- *Know your thoughts matter – think love and light.*
- *Know you are here for a purpose at this time on the planet.*

- *Know simple is best.*
- *Know you can make a difference, for the better, by shining your light of love.*
- *Know by speaking your truth you are claiming your personal sovereignty.*
- *Know to take special care of yourself first.*

A saying I came across recently states:

> "Once you accept life as it is, you relax. Instead of trying to change where the ball landed, you play the ball where it landed and go with the flow!" Unknown source

By breathing deeply and going with the flow may you have days of many delights in the simple things in your life.

THIRTY-FIVE

Negatives into Positives

In life we are forever having experiences that are upsetting; be they minor irritations through to tragic events. At these times, the universe is *creating* or *setting-up* our upset, drama, or disaster so we can learn and gain wisdom, often in hard ways.

The choices we make when in the middle of an upset, whether minor or major, helps us find tools to cope with and resolve the situation. Therefore, adding to our wisdom and enabling us to gather and integrate hard won inner strength.

Recently, with a dear friend, I was staying at my son's home in Margaret River while he was away. It was at the end of our cold, wet winter and the gas bottle that supplied the heating and hot water ran out of gas. My son had not expected us to be staying in his absence so had not considered this possibility. As it was the weekend, it was not possible to get a replacement gas bottle. After contacting him he suggested we have our hot showers at the Recreation Centre.

It turned out this minor upset led us to visiting the wonderful amenity of indoor swimming pool, basketball court and hot showers that we had not had cause to visit before. We chose to be adaptable and flexible and consider it an adventure. (Of course, we were also in need of hot showers!) By the way, I had brought a little electric radiator heater with me from Perth, so we were fine for house 'spot' heating.

We have sayings such as, *"Turning Negatives into Positives,"* *"Every cloud has a silver lining"*, and *"Something good comes from something bad."*

For example, without my marriage ending many years ago, I doubt I would have written my trilogy of books or begun spiritual counselling and coaching (through automatic writing), thereby assisting and inspiring many to understand more about themselves and the meaning of existence. It was all meant to be.

I have heard Paralympians comment that without their disability they would never have achieved so much or have had the opportunity to inspire so many. They turned their situation into one of triumph and fulfilment.

We all have free will and yet I feel we each have a destiny path to follow and the upsets, big or small, are the turning points for us to stay-on or get-on our selected path towards our *reason for being*.

Go well in noticing the signs guiding you on and trust the outcome.

THIRTY-SIX

Climate Change

Is extreme weather part of the new paradigm for our home, Earth, and humanity? As climate change shows itself at full force and the planet is in distress, so is much of humanity.

The wonderful, harmonious relationship between nature and human appears now to be so out of balance, with many people being totally disconnected from all the wonders of nature. And nature too is suffering badly. Communing with and having gratitude for all there is in nature is so vital. Many of us need to change the way we live and understand we are only able to live on this planet due to the divine orchestration of all players; flora, fauna, water, air, sunlight, minerals etc. Each plays their unique role to perfection and keeping the magical harmony.

Nature gives us loving support, healing and restores our balance and strength. By connecting to the earth (walk barefooted when you can) we ground ourselves to be more stable and content in this world. We are energy and it is vital to recharge, especially as many people wear rubber soled shoes cutting off this link to grounding and being renourished.

As I say in my book, *'Adventure into Transformation'*:

> *"... an exchange of love and comfort for mutual benefit takes place. Dramatic changes can take place in you, the plants, animals, and water, for example, when you give loving attention to them. Remember you and nature are one, intertwined with each other during your journey through existence on Earth."*

May you have enriching days, embracing nature more fully.

Do the seemingly small things, appreciate your house plants, place water in containers in your garden or on your balcony for the birds and the bees, encouraging them to visit. Plant more trees, enrich your soil with organic matter, make sure you have earthworms. Show your intention of being aware and give gratitude for all that is beautiful in your surroundings.

THIRTY-SEVEN

A Grand Design

"You are all higher entities walking on this planet, disguised as simple biological beings, and the disguise fools everyone – even you!"
Kyron (through Lee Carroll)

How do you react to the above statement?

Do you identify with the concept, or not?

There is a great deal to ponder upon. How you feel may be due to your awareness and understanding of who you are as a human. Whatever your level of acceptance of the statement is, know that you are much more than your seemingly three-dimensional self. We are all courageous, worthwhile souls here to have an experience as a human being.

The tests are continuing to challenge and help us grow into higher levels of consciousness. Are these tests part of a grand design?

My home country, Australia, and many countries around the world, have recently endured devastating wildfires over huge areas of precious land, with the losses of human life, animals, insects, and plants, changing and scarring the landscape for many years to come. Fortunately, these events have brought out the best of human nature with new levels of co-operation and kindness amongst local communities and people around the world. There has been a reconnection to the true value of life. The attention has returned to the preciousness of clean air, clean water and hopefully more love between us all.

Climate change is evident globally. Extremes of weather keep occurring; heat waves with higher temperatures than ever before, snow and ice melting at rapid rates with the permafrost in the Arctic releasing dangerous toxins into the atmosphere as it recedes, major floods, intense cold, devastating earthquakes, widespread fires -including across Siberia - also releasing carbon in the Northern Hemisphere summer of 2021. Mother nature is in distress.

Humanity has need to adapt to this shift in the environment along with the adjustment to higher frequencies of energy for our bodies to transform into a newer state of being. We are being challenged and tested at many levels.

As we move forward, stay grounded, be kind to all, and appreciate each beautiful day. Know all is as it is meant to be. Perhaps it *is* part of a grand design?

THIRTY-EIGHT
Wisdom and Grace

Wisdom and *Grace*: I consider these two words are representative of the values we can best live with – along with *Love*.

To have *wisdom* reveals we are highly conscious, aware, and awake to the nature of our journey as humans. With wisdom we can make the best choices and take informed action in all circumstances. This wisdom usually arrives for us after we have had many life experiences, sometimes painful and traumatic, and we have gone deep within ourselves to find resolution. We gain inner expansiveness of our knowing.

It is the letting go of our ego self as the prominent decider in our life and embracing our true higher self to be our guiding voice. This higher self does not need or seek approval from others. It has a knowing that we are unique and perfect as our individual self – we have no need to be influenced by mass or group thinking.

When we live with our beautiful personal wisdom, we will naturally live in a wonderful state *of grace*. With grace we have no need to be forceful, anxious, fearful, impatient or strive to fit in. We are also more kind, thoughtful, accepting, have empathy for others and gratitude for all we have!

Wisdom and grace together create a magical energy field that brings us the perfect environment, increasing our frequency and vibration, and allowing us to live more fully in the multidimensional reality of our new existence.

Many blessings – and a life full of grace, wisdom, creativity and love.

THIRTY-NINE
Sacred Geometry

My focus was jogged back to the intrigue and meaning of crop circles recently when I watched a documentary on this subject.

What is your understanding about them? Have you ever walked through one?

Early in 1995 I stayed with some friends in Beckhampton, near Avebury in England, during a visit to the UK and we walked amongst the ancient Avebury stone formations. I have never slept and dreamt so well as I did in my friends' home. They explained their home was built from the broken stones from the Avebury formation, which were created by the pagans in earlier centuries, and held powerful energies.

Interestingly, many of the incredible crop circle patterns have occurred in England near Avebury, Stonehenge and surrounds. There seems to be significant alignments and connections between the crop circles and sacred sites. Over the years there have been many hoax crop circles made by humans, and these tend to destroy the crops on which the patterns are formed. Whereas genuine crop circle crops are only bent into beautiful layers and later the crops can be harvested.

Authentic crop circles seem to be created very quickly by electromagnetic energy from another frequency and dimension of existence – a form of intelligence not from our planet. Many people who have entered these true crop circle formations have felt a powerful energy force emanating from them. Sometimes the colour of the skin on their hands changes when they place them on the flattened crops, headaches occur, and some people even fall asleep! Others have heard wonderful harmonic musical tones or been healed of an illness.

Are the amazing geometric patterns found in crop circles giving us messages, codes and symbols? Many of them are replicas of complex mathematical ratios in geometrical shapes, such as Sacred Geometry and Egyptian Metaphysics in the *Flower of Life crop circle* in Froxfield, in 1994. There have been many, many more with breathtakingly, complex designs.

Is it an attempt by the 'creator energy' of existence for us all to wake up to the greater purpose for being here on Earth? Or to know that we are not alone?

Perhaps pause and investigate these visual signs a little more.

FORTY

Ancestral Lineage

Every now and then I dip into finding out more about my ancestors through our family tree. At these times I have a strange, yet lovely, recognition factor which overwhelms me.

We are all unique souls who occupy a body however, we also have inherited our genes from our human forebears, and they can be great factors in our lives.

Communicating with both my maternal great-grandmother and maternal grandmother 'in spirit' a few years ago, they thanked me for having the courage to be independent from old expectations for the female lineage within our family line. They acknowledged me for liberating them through my actions, for speaking my truth, and theirs, and for being a creative authentic warrior acting on my inquisitiveness and not conforming to past patterns.

This has created healing for them all!

As already mentioned, my maiden-name is *McKenzie*. So, I travelled to the Highlands of Scotland a few years ago to visit the area around *Balintore Fearn*, a fishing village on the Cromarty Firth, to see my ancestral homeland. This was where my great-grandfather, Hugh McKenzie, was born and lived before he immigrated with his family to Australia in the 1850s seeking a better life.

Just by chance the *McKenzie / MacKenzie Highland Games* were being held nearby at *Castle Leod*, home of the chief of our clan, *the Earl of Cromartie*, John MacKenzie. I was honoured to meet him when I attended this truly special day and heard the fabulous bagpipes and watched clans' people in tartan kilts.

During this trip to Scotland, I also visited a memorial to the *Brahan Seer* (also known as *Coinneach Odhar* and Kenneth of Kintail) a 17th century MacKenzie from Lewis. The memorial is at Chanonry Point on the Black Isle, Cromarty Firth not far from where my great-grandfather lived. Brahan is the name of the castle, which is now a ruin, the seat of the MacKenzie clan at the time. He, sadly, was boiled in oil for supposedly dabbling in witchcraft, as well as his ability to *know* things and predict the future.

With my ability as a shaman, I identify with this very distant relative of mine. At times I can predict things and help find lost items. I first discovered I could do this accurately when, during a visit to New York, a friend of my lovely host asked, tongue in cheek, if I could tell her where her long-lost pearl necklace might be.

During some automatic writing I did the following day, I asked spirit this question and received the answer that the pearls were behind the chest of drawers in her bedroom. I had never been to her apartment, and I was just as surprised and delighted as the owner of the pearls when she discovered they were indeed there!

Acknowledging our lineage with gratitude hopefully gives us a determination to make the most of our life. As knowing that we have chosen our parents for a reason, we are correspondingly gifted with the DNA/genes we need to fulfill our mission in life.

Isn't this an empowering gift?

A JOURNEY OF THOUGHTS

I say it again: *"Know we are here at this time of existence to continue to fulfill the intentions of our ancestors in our genetic line. We are representing them and following on in bringing healing and greater awareness to this collective experience for humanity."*

Stay optimistic, inquisitive, and always claim your special personal sovereignty.

FORTY-ONE

The Beach

A few years ago, a very dear and much-loved friend, Margaret, passed away (transitioned) within three months of being diagnosed with cancer. Her grace, dignity and continuing concern for others during this time was beautiful to witness. Acceptance that this life was coming to an end brought peace during her last few weeks.

Her accomplishments were many. She never wavered in her service to others, even during times of personal hardship, illness and disappointment. She was a great events' organiser, with creative vision which went beyond standard planning practices, producing wonderful outcomes for fundraising events. All of this was done with gentle authority and a sense of calm.

Memories of her great love of the beach gave Margaret solace during her illness and she found comfort and joy in the following poem I had written. We both resonated with the words.

The Beach
Do you ever go to the sea and the sand?
The sparkling water at the edge of the land
It really takes my breath away
As I venture forth there every day

A JOURNEY OF THOUGHTS

Mercurial splendour at its best
Allowing my body to float and rest
Within its enveloping and tingling foam
I know I have found my sacred home

Do you love to spend time by the beach, a river or lake if you live close enough? It soothes the soul and is wonderfully healing!

FORTY-TWO

Do and Be Your Best

Og Mandino says, *"Always do your best. What you plant now, you will harvest later."*

So true! I add to this quote with the following:

Always be your best and become a different, better, and higher version of yourself.

As we experience life, we have many tests of initiation or challenges that tend to temporarily lower our vibrations. It is not the tests themselves, but our choices in dealing with them and then achieving wise outcomes that creates a *good pass*.

With wise choices we reinforce our best selves helping us once again to raise our vibrations to an even higher level of frequency. We update to our highest self.

We feel more serene, lighter, and have greater inner peace. Energetically, as we change, everything else around us shifts and adjusts to this new magnificent version of us. In doing so we step into the multidimensional version of ourselves and find we live with greater ease and grace – and are more creative and loving.

Achieving a sense of peacefulness is a big challenge. How can we find and hold that feeling? Changing priorities of focus in our daily routines will help.

Slow down, breathe deeply, detach, say, *"No"* where applicable, turn off the noise and distraction of television, other devices, unwanted stimulation and keep away from artificial light. Spend more time in nature, ground yourself, sit under a tree, plant a seedling, hug a tree. Reconnect with what sustains you. Listen to soothing music and the calming rhythms of nature.

Appreciate how amazing it is to have Earth as our home. Give it love, give love to yourself – and remember we are interconnected with the natural world. Our human health is closely connected to the health of the planet.

Stand in courage, keep laughing, be real – and be the example of a sovereign human who helps people to wake up out of their slumber. We are transforming into our new self.

Aim to be your shiniest and magical best self always.

FORTY-THREE

An Attitude of Love

The richness of the English language is never ending. The interpretation of words can be magical.

Looking at the word 'live' we are reminded of all we, as spiritual beings, are here in physical reality to do and be. We are here to *live*, and it is the *way we live* where the tests of initiation are found and progress along our path to transformation and deeper understanding is made.

As you remove *'i'* from the word *'live'* and replace it with the letter *'o'* the word transforms into the word 'love'. We can say 'i' is *ego* and 'o' represents wholeness, the completeness, the oneness of us all.

So, as you replace your own egocentric way of living with the beautiful universal attitude of oneness with all things, an attitude of *love* is created, naturally and graciously in all you are being and doing.

Love is the key to all living and within this word is a simple reminder for creating the best possible environment to achieve your purpose and path in life. As you surrender your personality (ego), recognising and allowing the divine plans to manifest for you, that are far grander than you can imagine, *you will find your purpose.* From this state the love will flow in fast and abundantly in all ways.

Can you create your future now, by letting go of fear and trusting the love essence that you are here to experience in your living?

Beyond the near future is no future, as we will all be in timeless reality where we will live our dreams and be part of multidimensional living, allowing us all to be where we wish by thinking and feeling love in all ways.

FORTY-FOUR

Multidimensional

The title of my first book is, '*The World Beyond Today – A guide to your multidimensional future.*'

I restate that the world beyond today is here now.

We need to be living multidimensionally to be in harmony with this changing world.

What is meant by *multidimensional*?

> *Three dimensional* is a term for the physical world of most humans, with the use of five main senses; seeing, hearing, smelling, touching/feeling and tasting. The sixth sense is intuition and knowingness, it is the bridge to your *multidimensional* ability. You can access your higher consciousness and link with universal wisdom. Being multidimensional allows you to access all facets of your being and gives a direct link with all that is – the creator of all life.

The paradigms of existence are changing rapidly and there is a new paradigm of being human. We need to open our awareness and embrace this change in human evolution and consciousness. By living multidimensionally we have greater empathy, compassion, a deeper appreciation of beauty, are kinder, more forgiving and caring. You can achieve this by listening to your intuition, noticing and acting on the signs and synchronicity in your life.

It is most important for us all to bring much needed light to life in this world.

As an explanation of multidimensional living, the wonderful author and medical intuitive Caroline Myss, PH. D, used the analogy of people living in an apartment building in a recent podcast. She described people living on the 1st floor of the building as having a limited view from their windows, while those living in the basement would have very little view at all! This can be compared to third dimensional living of mankind. We have accepted this reality.

However, many of us have already or are now taking the elevator up to a higher floor - say the 5th floor - where we have an expanded view from the windows. We are now in a multidimensional reality of truth with greater perceptions, perspectives and understanding. We now have a higher level of consciousness and a clearer picture of the landscape and our role in living. We remember and are more connected to our soul self who will reassure us of our reason for being.

Do not stifle your soul by staying on the 1st floor and having limited views and knowing. Be adventurous and expand your awareness by making an effort to climb the stairs or take the elevator to the 5th floor. Your perceptions will be elevated and wrapped in love as your knowledge grows regarding the meaning of life. We can say we are now in the 5th dimension of living where we have greater intuition and wisdom. Of course, you will need to have the curtains open to have the best view – even if you are higher up.

In becoming multidimensional, you will leave behind your old, limited thinking and being, and embrace all that is wiser and magical in this higher place of knowing.

Are you there yet – or busy riding the elevator?

Enjoy – and blessings for your new home.

FORTY-FIVE

Unconquerable

A few years ago, Australia hosted the *Invictus Games* in Sydney, NSW.

Their motto is: "I am".
Invictus means: "Unconquerable".

Those participating have shown how we can turn negatives into positives.

The Games' competitors demonstrate inner strength, honour and optimism as individuals who have been through their own 'dark night of the soul' and survived. Either experiencing mental or physical disabilities (or both) from time spent in military service, these extraordinarily courageous men and women have become, "Masters of their fate and captains of their soul." (quote from William Ernest Henly).

About five hundred participants from eighteen countries took part in many sporting endeavours. It was participation that mattered, not winning! It was the connection between souls, with hope and support.

Prince Harry, Duke of Sussex (United Kingdom) and patron of the Games, initiated them in 2014.

In his inspiring Opening Ceremony speech, Prince Harry said:

> *"It may be a different reality than envisaged (for the injured participants), none the less it becomes a reality that contributes to raising the consciousness of humanity, through your endurance, resilience and courage. No challenge is too difficult to overcome. It is ok to tell how we feel, it is ok to ask for help, it is ok to hug."*

These members of the Invictus Generation, as Prince Harry named it, are role models for the unconquered human spirit – I am Strong – I am Brave – I am Resilient – I am Not Alone

These amazing people will *not be* conquered.

May we all go forward with these positive and inspiring thoughts.

FORTY-SIX

The Gift of Grief

Grief: A powerful word and feeling.

Most of us have experienced the sadness of trauma and grief. Unfortunately, it is part of the human condition, and yet it can also provide us with an opportunity for huge growth in consciousness.

Grief can be encountered at the loss of expectation of how you think your life should be, the loss of choice and freedom, or the loss of someone close. While, children's first experience of grief can be through the loss of a much-loved pet, or their favourite toy, doll, teddy bear or security blanket. They need validation and comfort during this time just as we all do when grieving.

How do we process our grief?

Processing through the stages of grief vary and are unique for every individual.

They are all valid.

Shock, denial, anger, bargaining, depression and acceptance can all play out as the loss and grief is processed. Arriving at the acceptance stage allows the healing to begin, although the 'scars' usually remain at some level.

There can be collective community grief caused when a group within the community dies, such as in a car, plane, boating or bus accident. The same can occur through devastation caused through fire, flood, or cyclones/hurricanes. The coming together and the support of the people in the community can be very valuable as they all mourn together.

Many of my clients have experienced grief and loss of a loved one and through a session with me they can connect with, and gain messages of understanding, reassurance, and comfort from them in the spirit realm. It is part of the acceptance stage of knowing their lost loved one is only a thought away.

I encourage the client to then reach out, as time goes on, and find their own way to communicate with the departed loved one. Many have done this with great results.

Consciousness is expanded to an understanding that we are eternal, and it is only the physical body that has gone. Have you come to this realisation? Many in spirit are eager for us to connect with them and so begin a dialogue, bringing a wonderful richness and comfort to our life.

Intention and trust will bring success. Stay strong and loving always.

FORTY-SEVEN
Desirable Beliefs

The following statement by Bertrand Russell in 1953, was forwarded to me recently:

> *"Diet, injections, and injunctions will combine, from a very early age, to produce the sort of character and the sort of beliefs that the authorities consider desirable, and any serious criticism of the powers that be will become psychologically impossible. Even if all are miserable, all will believe themselves happy, because the government will tell them that they are so."*

How do you react to the above words? Do you identify with what was said?

It is of concern to many people that this statement, written so long ago, is stating what is now evident in our world.

Many believe there is abnormal control, conditioning, coercion, cruelty, and people are being misguided and deprived of truth. There is a loss of autonomy; a slow burn of loss of personal sovereignty with many people acquiescing too readily. There has been installation of fear (false evidence appearing real) with manipulation of humanity.

Why?

What is the hidden agenda?

Pay attention, do your own research, find the truth.

It is so important to be true to you, always claim and shine your light, think for yourself, question, and challenge all you are asked to do and be.

Wake up! Stay strong and loving.

Breathe.

FORTY-EIGHT

A Simple Life

During the past few years, I feel I have experienced an energy shift; a new vibration, a new frequency of being, a new level of consciousness.

It has been a time of small challenges, much reflection and going within.

I feel beautifully different, lighter, more trusting, accepting and detached. I feel I have let go of many old patterns and expectations.

Has this been your experience?

I feel I have more wisdom (hopefully) and insight into the cycles of life, with a greater understanding (once again, hopefully) of people's situations and struggles.

It is as though the 'protective' layers have been stripped away. I am now prepared to accept more fully my authentic self and be true to who I am and my reason for being.

There is more contentment in living a simple life, stripping away the unnecessary, with more appreciation of the joyful events that unfold when there are no expectations.

Magic occurs easily. Positive energy brings positive outcomes.

Perhaps the marvellous body work I have been having with a wise Chiropractor, as well as an open and grateful attitude, have contributed to this new me. It has unblocked the blocks that had prevented clearing of the old.

Remember we all create our own reality.

I have been fortunate to have the loving support of family and friends as well as being surrounded by the warmly embracing energy from the fabulous birds, trees, shrubs, and flowers in my garden. The environment is joyful and serene – a perfect place to live and replenish.

Step lightly into this changing energy. Act lightly, eat lightly, think lightly, love lightly. Then your light will shine even more brightly.

May each day bring you all that you wish to manifest for the greater good of all and yourself. In doing so we'll each contribute to a more loving, kinder, and more peaceful world.

FORTY-NINE

Forgiveness

Recently a dear friend phoned me and posed the question, *"How do I define forgiveness?"*

I intuitively responded to her question by saying that forgiveness can be attained when one is ready, having reached a level of deeper understanding and awareness. It is a wonderful and powerful universal teaching and learning for us all and allows us to grow. To define it I opened my second book, 'Adventure into Transformation' and looked for the topic Forgiveness to see what had been written by my wise guidance.

> I quote: *"Forgiveness is the ability to let go of hurts from actions by others who were part of your past experiences and learning. As you forgive these people, you free yourself to live in the present moment without hanging on to your wounds within ---. The action of forgiveness frees you from the bondage you still have with the persons concerned ----. In the forgiveness of others, we remind you to be very aware of forgiving*

yourself where necessary for past unkind or unloving deeds you have done to others or yourself ---. To forgive is to give your soul freedom to fly."

May the future bring you a lightness of being as you step from the shackles of being unforgiving to a new you, free of hurts and wounds.
Let go and be free!

FIFTY

Willingness

In my earlier books, I have written with the help of my messengers from *ILLANITIS*. Many people ask me to explain this. As I wrote my books through automatic writing, I did not understand this myself until much later. There are clues within the word Illanitis when you separate the letters and add an apostrophe and the letter 'd' in the appropriate places. (I explained this briefly earlier in this book).

It becomes I'll an{d} it is. *I will and it is.*

This place is within each of us. We have the ability, when we have the *will* power to manifest all we have come here as a human to do and be. The magic is within.

- Have willingness for reverence of nature and all existence
- Be willing to forgive
- Be willing to be grateful and kind
- Be willing to grow in awareness of the meaning of life
- Be willing to love and be loved

We are a planet of *FREE WILL*

- If it is to be, it is up to me
- We create our own reality
- As we think, so it shall be

The above three sayings are for us to be guided by if we are to manifest our highest potential.

We become more expansive when we open our hearts and minds to unlimited possibilities and continue to be optimistic in the way we live our lives.

We then attract all that we have scripted to be blessed with and have not blocked out (by negative thoughts and feelings) all that we deserve to have and be.

It is most important for us to retain our free will and our sovereignty in these changing times. Be an independent thinker, be authentic and lead a courageous life. Do not play it safe.

May you use your will for the highest and most beautiful of intentions and be the best *you* that you can be.

Many blessings for your continuing journey.

FIFTY-ONE

Animal Love

Do you have respect and gratitude for animals? Do you have an affinity with them?

Many of us have had and/or have pets in our homes now. Whether they be cats, dogs, mice, rabbits etc we tend to have them for companionship, joy and love. Children gain a sense of responsibility for their care and usually the rewards are immeasurable.

There is a unique connection between a human and animal companion. Most pets have a strong bond, loyalty and unconditional love for their owners and give company and sympathy when needed. Animals use telepathy to communicate and can be most supportive in times of great need; such as a cat sleeping on the bed with someone who is dying. They are helping with the sacred transition of that person.

We humans are part of the animal kingdom and we all play our unique roles in the oneness of existence. We are all necessarily assisting each other to grow in our consciousness, even though man has depended on animals as a source of food throughout time.

My own experiences, mainly with cats, have been magical. One evening during a meeting with a group of friends in my home when we were discussing our world being full of fear after the 9/11 event, a beautiful cat friend of mine arrived in the room with a live mouse. He proceeded to play with it. The mouse stood up on its tiny hind legs and looked the cat in the eyes as though it was saying, "I am not in fear of you!" The cat was startled by this brave little mouse who promptly scuttled to safety. Here was an example to us to dispel our fears.

During a trip to a game park in South Africa I was fortunate to encounter some beautiful white lion cubs in the wild. It was a magical experience. See the photo on my Facebook site. (facebook.com/merriene.scott)

More recently, I obtained and read the enlightening book, *'Mystery of the White Lions'* by Linda Tucker:[11]

> *"The white lions are revered as sacred messengers and Star Gods – they are symbols of hope and enlightenment. They are guardians of the human soul, and they invite us to reawaken our own souls, in order to protect our planet."*

I am so pleased I found this great book. It is crucial we protect these white lions and all other wild animals who are in danger of extinction.

I seem to resonate with the energy of cats (domestic and wild) although I also love dogs and have great respect for all animals. Enjoy your relationship with the animals in your life whatever they may be.

Recently I was honoured to have had highly acclaimed author Jennifer Skiff who wrote, *'The Divinity of Dogs'* and *'Rescuing Ladybugs'*, name my book *'Adventure into Transformation'* as one of her seven most loved books.[12]

Her powerful books share with the reader the magical connection humans have with both domestic and wild animals and how crucially important it is to eradicate the mistreatment and cruelty of all animals. We are equal participants in the precious harmony of existence. Much of humanity has not behaved well in this regard.

There are so many other wonderful and inspiring books to read about animals which educate and inform us as well as give us pleasure and comfort. One of these is a powerful book I also recommend, *'White Spirit Animals: Prophets of Change,'* by J. Zohara Meyerhoff Hieronimus.[13] It has helped my awareness grow about the plight of animals.

There is a poignant quote at the commencement of one of the chapters as follows:

> *"All creatures exist for a purpose. Even an ant knows what that purpose is – not with its brain, but somehow it knows. Only human beings have come to a point where they no longer know why they exist." Lakota John Fire Lame Deer (Medicine Man 1903 – 1976)*

Bless all animals with your love and an open heart.

FIFTY-TWO
Rescuing Ladybugs

Recently I completed reading the wonderful book, by author Jennifer Skiff, I mentioned earlier, *'Rescuing Ladybugs'*.[14] It is a most compelling read, awakening me further to the plight of animals throughout the world. The author is a precious and courageous friend of mine. Jennifer's encounters and then resolutions with animals in distress shows her determination to help these animals with whom we share this planet. There are also stories and testimonials of many passionate advocates who are rescuing and improving the lives of animals across the planet.

I feel this book is important reading for us all. The natural world is in deep trouble.

We need now, more than ever, to live in harmony and with kindness with all living creatures and plants.

The saying *'rescuing ladybugs or ladybirds,'* can imply that if you always rescue them you, of course, have an understanding and compassion towards rescuing, and have an affinity with all animals. Your level of consciousness is such that you know each of us is part of the oneness of being. It is so important to allow all living beings to play their part in the intricate workings of the universe to maintain crucial balance and harmony on earth.

A JOURNEY OF THOUGHTS

During one summer I met with Jennifer Skiff, and her two gorgeous dogs, for a lovely swim in the ocean and a walk on the beach. Naturally we discussed her new book, *'Rescuing Ladybugs'* and I shared with her how serendipitously I had found a ladybug on my hand the previous day, the first one for years. A sign from the universe that all is in alignment and magic is everywhere.

Ladybugs or ladybirds are well known as a sign of good luck. Treat them gently and of course rescue them when need be.

FIFTY-THREE
Wonder of Nature

A while ago I shared a wonderful holiday on the South Western Australian coast with some delightful friends. We stayed in Yallingup, near Margaret River, which has a most spectacular sweeping coastal landscape with rolling surf and sometimes enormous waves that are a surfer's delight.

The land above the beach has intriguing bush, prolific with wildflowers and flowering shrubs and trees at that time of the year.

My friends, with whom I shared this holiday, are *Bush Flower Essence Therapists* with wide knowledge of the rejuvenating and healing properties of wildflowers, shrubs and trees. We encountered wattles, kangaroo paws, orchids and grass trees amongst a variety of plants.

The wattle or Acacia, for example, can help us to be *worldly wise* with the key words being *alert, wise, mature, aware,* and *responsible.* So, it was good for us to stand next to the wattle for a while! Check out my photos on facebook.com/merriene.scott

Grass trees have always intrigued me. When I was young, we called them *Blackboys* (which is now considered politically incorrect). The official name is Xanthorrhoea Preissii, also known as Balga trees. They give us *the strength of the creative warrior.* So perhaps that is what I have always aimed to be; a creative warrior!

Appreciating the wonder of nature and spending time in it is magically therapeutic and uplifting. Even creating a small garden (as I have done) at your home and surrounding yourself with colourful flowers and shrubs is rewarding. My courtyard garden gives me great joy.

Here are a few excerpts from my book *'Adventure into Transformation'* – topic 'The Wonder of Nature':

> *"All components of nature resonate at their own frequency levels. Your own frequency level also varies, depending on your level of awareness and wakefulness. When you are at a high frequency of vibration, you can begin to communicate with the animals, trees and plants, rocks rivers oceans etc. --- An exchange of love and comfort for mutual benefit takes place. --- Give love and healing to all of nature and ask also to be shown how you can assist them to live in their highest potential. Remember you and nature are one, intertwined with each other during your journey through existence on Earth."*

Do you spend time outside by the ocean or stream, trees and flowers, even for a short time each day or week? It is beneficial to walk barefoot and sit on the ground for a few minutes each time to reinforce your sacred connection with our wonderful home – Earth. You will gain much support and love.

FIFTY-FOUR

Rowing Your Own Boat

Do you know of the traditional children's nursery song *"Row, Row, Row Your Boat"?*[15]

The words of the song are as follows:

"Row, row, row your boat
Gently down the stream
Merrily, merrily, merrily, merrily
Life is but a dream."

I like to think of it as a metaphor for life!

- We need to row (have intent, put in effort)
- Our boat (form/body)
- Gently (with kindness, grace and dignity)
- Down the stream (our life journey)
- Merrily (with love, happiness and optimism)
- Life is but a dream! (Our soul is having an experience in human form!)

A JOURNEY OF THOUGHTS

ROW YOUR BOAT

Perhaps you have realised, "If it is to be, it is up to me" (as I mentioned before).

We have our own boat (body/soul) we need to row ourselves. We have chosen to create our own circumstances and experiences from which to learn. It is only with effort and intent we will bring about manifestation and achievement.

GENTLY DOWN THE STREAM

The stream is our life path, so by living gently and kindly, we create a lovelier environment in which to journey it – and draw to us an easier path with less hurdles, rocks and hazards.

MERRILY

Merriment and joy lift our vibrations/resonance to a higher and finer level which creates more positivity and a lovelier lens for looking at and coping with life.

LIFE IS BUT A DREAM

We can say life is an illusion. It is a play, with us being lead actor and director after writing our own script. The real us is our soul, just playing a role!

I am attempting to live life with 'impeccable merriment' and truly represent my spiritual name Merriene (Merrie – ne).

Being authentic, kind, and merry will hopefully manifest for you an amazing richer life.

Shine your light and continue to "row your boat merrily down the stream".

FIFTY-FIVE
Being Human

There seems to be a great deal of intense disturbance happening in the world, continuously, and it is most important for all of us to stay grounded, positive, in harmony and balance.

It is crucial for us to stand in the truth of who we are and not be distracted or led away from what is authentic, pure, and beautiful in our reality.

I have a poem I wrote a few years ago to remind us. Here it is:

BEING HUMAN

Being human is a bold experiment
To live with magical, impeccable merriment
Creating fun, love and trust every day
Will send the fear far, far away

Elevate your soul above the density
Creating bliss with magical propensity
We are here to search and know
Take the risk, listen, act and grow

Within your heart the passion lies
Bringing the sparkle to your eyes
As we have the courage of our soul
The journey of creation will unfold

So, have the courage of your soul and create a wonderful world for yourself and others.

FIFTY-SIX
Recognition

Something so very long overdue and necessary is now happening in my home country of Australia.

Recognition of our First Nations indigenous people – the Aboriginal and Torres Strait Islander peoples – is finally occurring on a larger and more prominent level.

The indigenous people have been in Australia for over 65,000 years and the new settlers from many other countries have, mostly, never fully honoured and respected them. The new settlers arrived officially in 1788 and in the years since, these original First Nations people have not had the recognition they deserved for their wisdom, deep connection to their country and sense of place.

Now, at last, they are emerging from the dark shadows of a painful history during more than 230 years to a position where there is more understanding and appreciation for their vibrant creativity, spirituality, and great knowing.

Their music and art have impact, with their rock art at sacred sites, which is thousands of years old, needing to be protected. At last, their many languages (across approximately 500 different nations) are being revived and taught before they are lost forever. For example: 'Kaya' is an aboriginal word for 'hello' and 'welcome'. Indigenous names, where appropriate, are now replacing existing names for places, street names etc.

These people are one of the oldest living continuous cultures on the planet. Most of their knowing has been passed down from generation to generation for thousands of years through rituals, storytelling, and song lines. Much of this is captured in the most marvellous rock art and paintings.

I do hope you are honouring your indigenous people wherever you live and if you are indigenous, you are celebrating your unique self and finally claiming your rightful place on behalf of all your ancestors.

The gifts to all of us with this acknowledgement is the balance of 'beingness' being restored to a more rightful place. Recognition of these amazing, wise people is overdue, bringing with it an emerging of the great knowledge, strength, and resilience they hold.

Healing of country and people is occurring, and the new settlers are gaining so much from the rich wisdom these most honourable First Nations people have to share, breaking down prejudices of the past and creating the opportunity for healing for all.

FIFTY-SEVEN
Magic Happens

Albert Einstein said:

> "There are two ways to live your life. One is as though nothing is a miracle. The other is as though everything is a miracle!"

Magic and miracles happen every day.

Wonderful creativity, in its many forms, is all around us if we choose to look and see.

Tuning in to the higher level of ourselves brings to us the awesomeness of our existence. We are inviting in the incredible magical workings of the universe. We are then in sync, so to speak, creating the opportunity for 'harmonic convergence' of possibility that is waiting for us as we open to trust with a loving heart.

The universe provides when we align.

- Do what uplifts you
- Retrain your thinking to the infinite possibilities always awaiting you

- Recognise and acknowledge the signs of magic/synchronicity
- Reversing expected outcomes is always possible

I have had many experiences of magical happenings, from finding a white feather (a sign from an angel!) on the path in front of me just when I felt despondent about something, to bumping into someone I was thinking about and needing to contact or seeing the most incredible double rainbow after a difficult day.

Choose to make your future one of focusing on the awesomeness of the beautiful and magical nature of existence.

Be at peace with your wise, divine self, knowing you are never alone. Ask to live a magical life and trust it will be so!

FIFTY-EIGHT

Reflections

I wrote this piece at the time of my birthday, and I have been fortunate to have had many! I have mixed emotions as a result of the vast array of amazing experiences during my life.

For each of us it is a day of reflection. We are here celebrating another human lifetime (my belief) having chosen to be here to raise our consciousness through the experiences we have had and are having.

We can ask ourselves:

- *Have I chosen wisely in the way I have lived?*
- *Have I been kind, thoughtful, loving, and generous and contributed to the betterment of humankind?*
- *When I leave this world will I be satisfied I have achieved what I came this time to do?*

I feel it is wiser to have taken risks, been adventurous, open and flexible to new ideas, tolerant and compassionate when dealing with tricky situations rather than playing it safe and fearing change. Of course, unfortunately, I have played it 'safe' many times.

Perhaps you are here to overcome fear, guilt, deep anger, bitterness, or some of the myriad of other challenges of life. Every week we are faced with more horrors and sadness in the world reflecting the confusion people have in their lives.

It certainly is a time of shifting paradigms. We need to question our deep truth and live with goodness and understanding that we are all unique and precious in our differences and yet all equal and part of the oneness of being.

Be joyful and loving every day.

FIFTY-NINE
Moral Compass

Have you clarified and measured your moral compass?

With, *'right thought, right speech, and right action'*, a basic teaching of Buddhism, we are liberated to live with less angst and more peace.

Ask yourself these questions:

- *Do I live with stoicism in times of adversity?*
- *Do I overcome adversity and obstacles with grace and gratitude?*
- *Do I act to fit-in with the crowd or speak and act my truth?*
- *Do I always have to win an argument even if I know I may be wrong?*
- *Do I live each day as gloriously as I can with an attitude of humbleness, kindness, generosity, and love, contributing towards a more harmonious existence for us all?*

When my (then) fifteen years old, wise and serene granddaughter visited me a few years ago from New Zealand, she gave me insights into the priorities and thinking of intelligent teenagers. Their social media connections and concern for the world environment is hopeful.

She is now at university and contributing to new thinking for a better future for humanity.

This generation are the leaders of the future, with the huge responsibility to care for and perhaps save our planet from destruction. With the deep concern of many young people there is a glimmer of hope that we can begin to heal and repair this precious home of ours.

So, relax, have less angst and more peace and love in your thought, speech and action and do what you can to make the world a more beautiful place.

SIXTY

We Are What We Think

"We are what we think. All that we are arises with our thoughts. With our thoughts we make our world!"

The Buddha

The above quote is a powerful reminder that we create our own reality.

Are you a victim or a gloriously empowered being? Do you see your cup half full or half empty? We have the choice. We write our own script for our 'play' of each life.

A while ago I wrote a poem which describes and reinforces my intent each morning:

Today
As I lie in my soft and beautiful bed
The whispering winds fill the thoughts in my head
The pale pink sky of the coming morn
I do enjoy this time just before dawn
Today I know will bring joy and fun
Perhaps today I will play in the sun
The chirp of the birds so full of elation

Fills the air as part of creation
And today will also bring all kinds of love
All I need do is ask for help
From the wondrous angels above
No matter what happens
The choice is all mine
All I need do
Is trust the Divine

No matter what is happening in the world at this moment, enjoy each day as you can, with a loving heart and positive thoughts.

SIXTY-ONE

Changing Paradigms

I have just completed re-reading Barbara Marciniak's powerful book, *'Path of Empowerment'*. I mentioned this book in Chapter 28, 'Creating Miracles'. The book is full of wise insights into our reasons for being here on the planet at this turbulent time. She writes:

> *"Humanity creates the world at large by way of unconscious primal mass agreements. You are participating in a mass agreement that is exploring the nature of reality from a 3-D vista, and you contribute to energizing the collective experience into being through telepathy and* dreaming ...
>
> *You are a pioneer preparing a path for a new interpretation of reality."*[16]

Mass consciousness *is* now changing. Old paradigms and beliefs are disintegrating, hence the 'rising up' of millions of people protesting to create new paradigms.

Believe in your dreams, listen to your knowing, think independently, meditate, have times of peaceful silence. Have a positive attitude and an open heart.

Know we are here at this time of existence to continue and fulfil the intentions of our ancestors in our genetic line. *We* represent them and follow on in their footsteps to bring healing and greater awareness to this collective experience for humanity.

It is courageous work.

> Remember - we manifest our thoughts into being.
> Remember - we create our own reality.
> Remember - we are multidimensional.

Go forward with love – not fear.

SIXTY-TWO

We Are Nature

I have discussed this previously and wish to reinforce its importance.

With so much destruction and misery in the world it is vitally important for our wellbeing for us to focus on and appreciate the beauty of nature. Nature in all its forms reminds us we are *part of it*, not separate from it. The wonder and magic are evident if we care to look and notice.

An exhibition called, *'Frontier Surfing'* was held at the Fremantle Arts Centre in Western Australia a few years ago. It featured huge blown-up photographs, one by my son Jamie, of giant waves surfed by courageous and talented surfers. The power and magnificence of the water in motion in these images is breathtaking. See Jamie's photo with both of us in front of it on my Facebook page: facebook.com/merriene.scott

All of those who love surfing have a spiritual connection with the water and the challenge they face each time they ride a wave brings them into alignment with their reason for being.

Damon Hurst, the co-curator of the exhibition says: *"Frontier Surfing brings together a story of challenge and braveness but also taps into the humanity and singular spiritual connection between surfer and wave."*

Damon has since been instrumental in creating a wonderful permanent exhibition of Big Wave Surfing photos, taken by my son Jamie Scott, within the magnificent new Boola Bardip (Many Stories) Museum in Perth, Western Australia. A great honour for them both.

Most of us do not wish to go to such extremes as big wave surfing. However, whatever way suits you to tap into the natural force field of nature will enrich, rebalance and calm your spirit.

My love of swimming helps me to stay grounded, clear and joyful. I love the salt water so my choice is to swim in the ocean when the weather is warm. In the winter, I walk along the beach and through the shallow water to absorb a little bit of the salty water into my skin. I do this when I can and it helps me to continue to be grounded and joyful! Bare feet on sand are such a delight – and important for us to keep ourselves connected to Mother Earth.

SIXTY-THREE

Purity and Love

Glancing out of my living room window as I write this, my eyes are drawn to a beautiful full-blown, perfumed white rose proudly displaying itself on my one and only potted rose bush. There is a tightly closed rose bud nearby as a companion awaiting its time to reveal its beauty in a few days.

These are the last of the many, many exquisite white roses that have bloomed during the long flowering season giving much pleasure and joy to everyone here – nature is truly amazing!

I love and vibrate magically to white roses (see my Facebook page for my white rose photo: facebook.com/merriene.scott). They are a vibration and energy of purity and love. This is my intention to convey as I work with clients, which is apt with my shamanic name 'White Rose'.

We each vibrate in our own unique way. We each have our own unique fingerprints and signature, and we all know when we feel in harmony (or disharmony) with someone, some situation or place.

So, recognise and stay true to yourself and your unique vibration. Life will flow more easily for you when you do. It is the language of the heart.

Joy and sparkling vibrations always.

SIXTY-FOUR

Decluttering the Brain

Recently I was reminded by a colleague about how important it is to clear out the clutter in the brain - it can change our thinking.

We use our minds continuously and often restful sleep is difficult as our minds keep chattering to us. It can be most exhausting and prevents us from having the clarity to move forward in our lives in the best possible way.

If we clean out old unnecessary thinking, past patterns and habits of doing and being, it will be easier to clean out our physical 'stuff' as well. Restful sleep will help clear out our brain as will regular deep breathing, bringing in more oxygen.

Neuro (brain) plasticity (a word more widely known these days!) is a powerful and achievable ability, with intention and discipline, to change the workings of the brain.

We are what we *think* and so it is most valuable to *let go* all that no longer serves us. Clarity of thought brings clarity of action and being. So, when we can see something, or someone, is cluttering up our valuable energy we need to let it or them go. The patterns we create in our daily habits can be changed and this brings in a whole new set of circumstances, making room for new opportunities and manifestations to occur. The vibrations change.

A JOURNEY OF THOUGHTS

Brain clutter often occurs because we are continuously bombarded with sensory overload, from digital devices, social media, loud noises, traffic, television ads etc. It is important to be still, be quiet, meditate and spend time in nature as often as possible to allow our true vibrations to be nurtured, rested, realigned, balanced and uplifted so we can be in touch with our core truth.

Stay detached from other people's dramas, they are not your responsibility (unless close family or friend). Give them kindness, compassion and love from a distance.

Your brain will be grateful for a 'spring clean' and will help you gain a higher level of consciousness with a new level of creative and independent thinking.

As you think, so you shall be!

SIXTY-FIVE

A Deeper Declutter

My decluttering continues.

Now I have completed the sorting of the letters, photos and keepsakes of my dear mother who departed a few years ago, I am continuing with my own necessary clearing out that I mentioned earlier.

The process has been energy shifting and emotionally challenging as well as cleansing and freeing. Files are now being emptied of so much old and now unnecessary information from other long-gone chapters of my life.

It has been quite a shock and surprise to witness the long-forgotten paper statements of my endeavours, various careers, trips, bank balances, tax returns, investments etc, reminding me of those times and situations. Some were from as long ago as thirty years. Have you had similar feelings if you have done a big clean out?

Yet, I am grateful to have had such a rich and varied life with so many wonderful opportunities and experiences, along with good health. Now it all seems like a strange dream (sometimes a nightmare) with feelings of detachment from all I achieved back then.

A JOURNEY OF THOUGHTS

I keep reminding myself the *me* I am now, is the culmination of all I have experienced so far in this life and my hopefully increasing wisdom is due to all that happened earlier.

The struggles, disappointments, traumas and sadness, that most of us have at some stage, along with the joy, fun and experience of being loved and loving have contributed to the melting pot of 'what is'.

I now have a lighter feeling moving forward knowing each *now* will not be burdened by my paper clutter from the past. I can't wait to complete this task, and I may even have some empty shelf space in my study.

There is a saying (not entirely accurate here), *"Only when we discard our one remaining possession – our backpack – will we be entirely free!"*

By practising the law of detachment from all we have been attached to through our life we can more easily move into an energy of beautiful change and newness. These ideas, feelings, possessions and people have served us well in the past and were of value.

Have gratitude and now allow room for all of value that is here for you in the present.

SIXTY-SIX

Merriment

Occasionally I have mentioned *'impeccable merriment'*.

It is important to live with humour and now is the time, more than ever. Our world, for many of us, has been turned upside down so it is vital to keep our vibrations high and not be in fear.

One way of achieving this is to retain our sense of fun and laugh often if we can.

Going through another box of papers as I declutter, I came across the following words received from spirit through automatic writing. At the time, I was at a weekend away with a precious *'Conscious Creatives Group'* in 2002. This message (unchanged) is as relevant now, as time has no measure in spirit:

"Good morning, dearest Merriene, this is Joy, and I am the collective voice of all that is beautiful and pure. We are with you now to bring about a message of peace and hope for those of humanity willing to bring about the changes necessary. We wish you well, with the intent you have as a group, to change the dynamics of healing powers within the consciousness of man.

As you progress in your intent, you will be offered further assistance and advice from the highest office of all that is - and know you are bringing about the very beauty of existence with all you are being and doing. We bless you all as your quest gathers momentum. Trust the steps and stages are all perfect in their attainment and all is well with the ways of being.

We suggest you all bring forth your merriment as often as possible and lift the vibrations to a level of impeccability. Impeccability is vital now in this wonderful work you are achieving. Perhaps you will now bring about a mass education of those willing and awake enough to follow your footsteps.

All is in transition as you understand – and with the coming of further tragedies your own energies will be called on to brighten the light even further. Thank you for this opportunity to share with you, our thoughts.

Create beauty in all you think, do and are. We leave you now with the unfoldment about to come about. Hold your truths high, with great impeccability."

SIXTY-SEVEN

The New Children

It was a delight to have my elder son, daughter-in-law and three beautiful grandchildren with me briefly again in Perth. They were returning from a nearly three-month-long camping trip in the Kimberley area of Northwest Australia, before they ventured to their home in New Zealand.

The experiences they had, immersed in the splendour of this vast area of spectacular nature, will now be imprinted in them all for the rest of their lives. Away from all the trappings of modern life they were able to be fully connected with what is truly important. Following is a poem I wrote about the new generations of children such as my grandchildren.

The New Children
Joyful children everywhere
Living life without a care
Pure and innocent as they grow
Not remembering what they know
And yet they do remember as they think afar
A little of who they really are
For experiences anew to begin

A JOURNEY OF THOUGHTS

They need adjustment to their kin
So, as you look into their eyes
The wise souls they are, you will recognise
One day soon they will lead the world
Towards a new humanity that is strong, wise and bold
Celebrate with them their roles to come
Humanity is safe with these younger ones
Today, tomorrow and days after that
Bringing us to a new and wondrous habitat

SIXTY-EIGHT
Wise Choices

It has been said, *"It is not what happens to us in life but how we handle what happens to us."* We have free will and choice. I know at times I could have made wiser choices however this is how we learn and gain wisdom. The way we deal with problems is what is important. If we are wise, the greatest problems can lead to our greatest insights.

As an example, my son Digby had recently returned to his home in New Zealand after his annual wave sailing trip to the remote wilderness sheep station at Gnaraloo, 150kms north of Carnarvon, Western Australia. It is at the southern end of the magnificent Ningaloo Reef, which rivals the Great Barrier Reef for its beautiful coral, tropical fish and surf. Understandably, it is loved by surfers and wave sailors from all over the world for its natural beauty and isolation.

On this recent trip, two of Digby's group became lost when they sailed much further north parallel to the coast than they intended. They had missed spotting the vehicle on the shore that had been left for them to return to camp. Unfortunately, the coastline in this area appears to have few distinguishing landmarks when out on the ocean.

A JOURNEY OF THOUGHTS

Back at camp, the remaining group realised something was amiss when these two didn't return and alerted the emergency and safety authorities, via the station owners. A search and rescue plane was sent from Perth (about 1,000kms away) as well as a team of police from Carnarvon, to look for the missing sailors. As this was happening the sun was setting magnificently and the super full moon was rising simultaneously. A powerful and rare energy occurrence.

Digby and some others of their group set off on foot from the last accessible place to the beach for a four-wheel drive vehicle, armed with water, food and dry clothing. They left two friends behind at camp to connect with in case the missing wave sailors arrived back or were found, although mobile phones etc do not work in this isolated area.

Digby and the crew walked unsuccessfully for many kilometres, but there was no sign of the missing men. My son said, even though the situation was serious, the atmosphere was magical with the glorious full moon and the shimmering reflections in the water and on the wet sand as they walked.

The missing two were eventually found at different times and different locations with a great deal of effort and huge expense! The lost sailor closest to camp had initially walked north, and after about one kilometre realised his mistake and began walking inland to find a road. He was found about four hours after his designated return time. He had made a wise choice! The search plane with its infra-red camera located the other sailor and directed the searchers to him, via satellite phone, around midnight. He had landed further north and begun walking south along the beach for about six hours including rest stops. After four hours of walking, dehydrated and lost, he eventually set off his personal locator beacon which had triggered the alert for the plane. He said he had not wanted to set it off earlier and cause unnecessary trouble!

The sailors had not kept to the golden rule of *sticking together* when in the water. One had kept sailing when the other had stopped to fix some gear on his board.

Much wisdom was gained from this drama and exposed the wise and poor decision-making abilities of a group of men (and one woman) in this remote and idyllic location. Thankfully there was a happy outcome.

As we have our life experiences it is good to remember to act/react with the wisdom of our soul. Each *upset* is a *set up* to help us make thoughtful choices and elevate our level of consciousness.

SIXTY-NINE

Your Calling

Returning from another wonderful stay and energy-shifting time with my son and family in New Zealand, life once again presented itself with new activities to embrace.

On my plane journey home, I found myself sitting next to a lovely young Italian Monk returning to Italy after spending two years (with only two other Monks) in a Buddhist Monastery in Wellington, New Zealand. Sitting in this confined space - as you do in economy seating - we discussed much about the meaning of existence. During our flight, he shared his observation and practise of the importance of the mind and mindfulness. How the mind is so powerful in how we choose to be and do. Meditation is the key!

He commented how he spent many years searching, in India and elsewhere, to find his calling until he recognised and resonated with Buddhism. He had many challenges, times of great solitude and difficulties on this path. He had also lived a so-called normal life for years as a 'hippie' with long hair, loved parties, modern music etc as he searched. Now he knew this was where he was meant to be, and the rewards were in his great service to humanity. It was such an honour to share time and space with him.

We are all unique and each of us has our own different calling each lifetime.

We have a deep knowing, usually for what gives us joy, a feeling of alignment with our truth and what we need to do, be and become.

Our soul remembers why we have returned/rebirthed to live another life – as well as what our mission/contract is – and what we have agreed to experience and achieve each time.

As we align with our purpose, recognise it and act on it, we will indeed feel at peace.

So, whatever you feel is your purpose, embrace it, enjoy it and know you are fulfilling your reason for being.

SEVENTY
Uniting

Some time ago I was most fortunate to see the excellent movie, '*A United Kingdom*'.[17] It tells the story of the true-life romance and marriage of *Prince Seretse Khama* of Bechuanaland (now Botswana) and Englishwoman *Ruth Williams,* in the late 1940s.

Prince Seretse was due to be pronounced King on his return from his studies at Oxford University in England. Meeting in Oxford, their union faced fierce opposition from the British Government, tribal elders and the Apartheid Government of South Africa.

Fortunately, Seretse and Ruth defied and overcame all opposition to ultimately triumph with the love and support of the people of Bechuanaland (Botswana). Serendipitously, the news of the discovery of diamonds in their country gave them the power to stand alone as a couple, and with their nation and not be beholden to Britain or South Africa.

He went on to become became 1st President of Independent Botswana. One of their sons, Ian, was also President of Botswana in later years (2008 – 2018).

Seeing the movie with a dear friend, whose uncle was a friend of Prince Seretse at Oxford, made the story even more meaningful to us both.

Why am I sharing this with you? This is a fine example to us all about *uniting*. We are here on the planet as souls having an often very challenging experience as humans and we need to support each other on our unique journeys.

However, with what is now happening in the world there are more attempts to *divide* us even further apart.

From my perspective we need to draw on our wisdom, love, courage and kindness to all others and ourselves more strongly than ever.

Shine the light that you are.

SEVENTY-ONE

The Soul's Music

Music is food for the soul.

It is the basis in all our lives whether it is in the rhythms and sounds in nature such as bird song, the breeze rustling leaves in the trees, the beat of our hearts, the waves breaking on the shore, the sound of a tinkling brook, or man-made music in all its forms. Music is all around us and it is important for us to choose wisely in what we listen to.

A while ago I completed a reading of my book club selection, *'Music and Freedom'* by Zoe Morrison.[18] It has a powerful theme of the transformative powers of music and love. It got me thinking once again of the way music affects all of us. Then to synchronise this thinking I received an invitation, from a dear friend, at an hour's notice, to attend a wonderful classical music concert at the Perth Concert Hall! The concert featured world renowned conductor *Asher Fisch* and the fabulous pianist *Jean–Yves Thibaudet* who has performed around the world for more than thirty years. Music by *Mendelssohn, Saint-Saens* and *Gustav Mahler* enthralled the audience with the powerful and uplifting rhythms. What an amazing night.

In my book, *'Adventure into Transformation'* I have written:

> *"You enhance your transformation as you choose to listen to beautiful music whenever possible. With wonderful tones and rhythms, you bring your body and soul into perfect vibration, resonating in harmony with all that is the purest in sound and of the highest ...*
>
> *All beautiful music has its origin in the essence of angels. They bring forth the inspirational sounds that reach the composers of your music, so that your ears and feelings recognise those patterns of resonance that heal and soothe."*

It certainly can rebalance, uplift and comfort us. Music is powerful and magical.

To once again reinforce my thoughts, just prior to writing this I picked up the copy of my recently arrived Royal Automobile Club (RAC) magazine and spied an article titled, *'Can Your Music Choice Affect Your Driving?'* The researchers discovered that drivers who drove with easy-listening music, as opposed to drivers who listened to fast-paced music with vocals, were associated with the lowest level of driver errors.

So, make time for engaging in wondrous upliftment and healing with your selection of divine music.

SEVENTY-TWO

Good Vibrations

It is important for our vibrations to be compatible to create harmony with our surroundings and the people in our lives. A while ago I wrote a poem regarding finding a vibration to suit us individually. Here it is:

Your Radio
If you are feeling sad and low
Turn the dial of your radio
That is, the radio within
Within us all, where truth begins
Find a station that vibrates light
The secret to your happiness and might
Within are frequencies sublime
So, find the one of the loving kind
Meditation, fine music and good books
This is where you need to look
Being in nature, by water and trees
Helps for you to feel the breeze

The breeze of change to your vibration
At last, you will have found
Your perfect station

    We have free will to create and change our reality. We do not need to remain stuck with where we are by listening to the wrong radio station. We have the power to change and transform ourselves and be the best we can be and accept only the best. Become a higher vibration and enjoy compatible energies.

    Enjoy being who you deserve to be – the best!

SEVENTY-THREE

Know Thyself

The ancient adage, *'Know Thyself'* is a timeless instruction directing us towards a greater understanding of our connection with reality in the third dimension.[19]

As I have talked about previously, we need to expand our thinking and be curious, creative, and passionate. To change our reality to one of greater depth and meaning and where we can contribute with our unique truth.

'Know Thyself,' is also the motto of the college where I trained and graduated as a teacher. During that training I was not so aware of how profound a statement this is.

My first posting as a teacher was to Serpentine, a little town not far from Perth, Western Australia. Kundalini energy (known as our life force energy) is serpent-like and connected to the spine. Interestingly, our ancient selves were of reptilian heritage. As you can see, I like to see the connections between things.

I now know the area of Serpentine is a spiritual portal. There were hidden clues (in my interpretation) and designs in these happenings leading me on in my life.

To *know thyself* we need to accept ourself as a magnificent, unique being in human form having an experience as this identity or personality we have chosen to be this lifetime. It takes courage and deep exploration to be comfortable being who we are. We will claim our knowing of our role, perhaps after much trauma and bewilderment, when growing up. Eventually, if we do the work, we will then find our peace.

Of course, there are many levels or layers of knowing and it is only through much searching within that we can claim our sovereignty.

Shine your light with love, knowing yourself as a unique and magical energy.

SEVENTY-FOUR

Angels

Many years ago, when I was new to the exploration of spiritual matters, I attended a channelling evening where it was suggested that we each had our own special angel with us that evening and to intuit its name.

The name '*Perpetua*' popped into my head and immediately I dismissed it as the angel's name. Later I realised this was the perfect name for my visiting angel and of course we are never without our beautiful angelic guidance. They are forever with us to support, protect and inspire.

Do you have a name for your angelic guidance?

If not, sit quietly and ask. A name will come to you. When talking to your guidance, using a name is similar to having a pin code, giving you quick access to this wonderful, sacred source of wisdom and comfort.

We are never alone, so enjoy each day with this knowledge of your greater self and all to which you have access.

Following is a conversation I had with Perpetua shortly after I found her name:

> *"Dear Merriene,*
>
> *I am your very own angel of love and light and my name Perpetua you have chosen, as you and I have been permanently together since 'time' began – and my role now will become more active in this present reality of being ...*
>
> *I can best describe my energy as one with God and all that is in existence. I am part of the God energy, and my divineness is one with you.*
>
> *We are pure energy, and our beauty together will touch the souls of those who come into our field ...*
>
> *Our task is to be the messenger and the healer of many souls. We can make them aware of their own divineness and beauty and show them the way home ...*
>
> *I will be the overlying presence with you ..."*

No matter if you believe, or not, we all have assigned to us our helpers 'beyond the veil', or back curtain in our play on the stage of life. They give us inspiration, protection and reassurance. They often come in our dreams and intuition, so remember and take note of the messages you receive in this way.

SEVENTY-FIVE

Riding the Waves

Below are some thoughts I had in a creative writing session:

"I am a champion surfer of waves on the ocean. I was born knowing this and yet as I was born, I didn't find the circumstances allowing me to do this. It took me a long time to find a wave to train on and find a coach to remind me how to do it.

However, in my time of waiting I learnt many other new things from family, friends and strangers around me. I learnt patience, tolerance, determination and how to fit in and compromise. I also learnt about frustration and unfairness and how most of humanity is unwilling to stretch beyond the known paradigms of being and doing.

After many eons of experiencing life away from the beautiful waves, my opportunity came to take to the water. I began riding small waves to strengthen my always healthy body and discovered many other people who have a similar passion. I could see those grand surfers on larger waves riding them with grace and ease, avoiding the sharp reefs and turbulent unpredictable waves. They had discernment and self-belief in what they were achieving. This is what I knew I wanted to do, and could do, as I built up my strength, courage, belief and fitness.

So eventually I took to the grand and powerful waves and discovered great joy in the ability to ride and accomplish this journey on each wave. The waves I ride now are waves of change and in letting go of any fear of where each wave will land - and with no expectations what I will find there - I trust each glorious wave will bring me to a place of love and joy, with the hope this will inspire others to dare to ride their own challenging waves!"

How are you going in riding your waves?

SEVENTY-SIX

Endings and Beginnings

Sometimes challenging events happen at crucial times in our lives to assist us to let go, forgive, and open our hearts to new situations, arrangements and ideas.

They create paradigm shifts.

Our lives are full of change and the more we embrace it when it occurs the easier it is to adjust to the new.

The death of a dear cousin, the welcome birth of a lovely baby girl to my much-loved nephew and his wonderfully serene partner, and most precious time with my two sons, partners, and fun grandchildren during the holiday season has opened my heart further to both sadness and great joy.

It has been a time of endings, beginnings and stronger connections with loved and valued family members and friends.

Have you had a chance to reflect on all that has occurred for you during the months of this year? With a new vibration it is as though we need to reset our perspectives, values, and intentions with a greater resolve.

Life experiences and stages seem to go in a circular fashion, or more accurately – in a spiral, and run their course. Or we could say we have chapters or acts 1, 2, 3 etc and as each chapter or act ends, we can move on to our new challenges, lessons and circumstances.

It is healthy to recognise this and be willing to part with the old so we can move into the new. We would not wish to continue to be in primary school or high school forever – we are in *life school* - and it is important to invite in our new level of experiences and learning.

By honouring past scenarios and people in our life we will retain the value and impact of those times and carry this wisdom with us into our present reality. It is part of the colourful tapestry of our life journey.

A shift in the archetypal pattern in the world is happening with the recent passing of Queen Elizabeth II of the United Kingdom. We are experiencing an energy shift of Cosmic magnitude. It is the end of an era. It is a new beginning.

The Queen embodied the Queen archetype fully for her long reign of seventy years. She can now rest after fulfilling, with duty and responsibility, and at the highest level, her big soul contract.

There were many beautiful signs of confirmation at her transition:

- She passed away at Balmoral in Scotland where she felt most at peace. I have been told it is *the Earth Star Chakra* – the Solar plexus and the anchor of power.
- The alert code to pass on when she died in Scotland was *Operation Unicorn*, a powerful 7th dimensional frequency.
- She died on *Mother Mary Feast Day.*
- There was a magical *double rainbow* - forming a bridge for Prince Philip to greet her - and a *single rainbow* over her other home Windsor Castle at the time she died. A great blessing.
- It *rained* on the day she left – which is also a great blessing.

- The *amazing queue* where people stood for many, many hours to pay their respects to her as she lay in state. It was a message of *love in action* and gratitude for all she represented.

On a visit to Perth, Western Australia in 2011, Queen Elizabeth II mentioned the following in her speech:

"We are all visitors to this time, this place. We are just passing through. Our purpose is to observe, to learn, to grow to love and then return home."

I am sure she feels well pleased, now she has returned home, for fulfilling her destiny path and role so admirably.

May we all fulfill our own destiny path and contract with as much grace and honour.

SEVENTY-SEVEN

Seasons

The different seasons bring opportunities for change and appreciation of the wonder of nature, renewal, and fresh thinking.

I must say I do enjoy the warmer weather and so I am delighted to see little signs of the arrival of spring, after winter, here in the Southern Hemisphere. The fresh budding of trees and flowers and the longer days are magical.

There are orderly designs of nature. We need to have a greater empathy with *all* forms of life rather than be separate from them.

David Suzuki and Peter Knudtson wisely state in their great book, *'The Wisdom of the Elders'* as follows:[20]

> *"The ancient, culturally diverse aboriginal consensus on the ecological order and the integrity of nature looks upon the totality of patterns and relationships at play in the universe as utterly precious, irreplaceable and worthy of the most profound human veneration."*

This is a profound truth we can all do well to have a willingness to live by.

The truth of human veneration of nature was realised during a wonderful communication I had with a tree when on a visit to an old growth forest in 1999. I was with a group of concerned, aware people during a rally to save our precious forests from being logged in the south west of Australia.

Firstly, I had hugged this magnificent tree and listened to what it had to say. It replied through clairaudience. I then quickly went to find pen and paper and asked for the message again.

Here is the message:

> "We are the energy of the tree you hugged, and we are connected to all trees ... We are so happy you give of your time and love to be with us today. We have great need of your love and concern, and we wish for you to speak out for us – as you will in the future. Please understand our need is for our time to live as trees in your eco system and to bring balance and harmony to the planet. Mankind do not, on the whole, understand the necessity for balance and you, as a species, need to respect the part you play is one of connection with all things ...
>
> Thank you for your attention. Please enjoy all of us and breathe easy here."

The tree of your hug.

Another powerful book with a theme on trees is the Pulitzer Prize winner for fiction for 2019, *'The Overstory,'* by Richard Powers.[21] I recommend you read it.

May you treasure all trees and understand they are sentinels of love and healing for us.

SEVENTY-EIGHT
Questions

As each year comes to a close, I reflect on my achievements of the past year.

I have asked myself the following questions, and you may wish to do the same:

Am I

- *Being my authentic self?*
- *Immersing myself in nature as often as possible?*
- *Being kind – to myself, other people, animals, the environment?*
- *Being forgiving?*
- *Living simply – and decluttering enough?*
- *Going within to have a richer relationship with myself?*
- *Being grateful for what 'is' and not complaining about what 'isn't'?*
- *Clarifying and implementing my moral compass?*
- *Moving to a higher and more aware vibration and level of consciousness?*
- *Claiming my power – my right to be my unique self?*

- *Being respectful of everyone else and their right to be their unique self?*
- *Remembering I am a spiritual (soul) being having a human experience?*
- *Having fun – and not taking life too seriously?*

Live in this now moment with impeccable merriment, choose your friends with discernment.

SEVENTY-NINE

The High Road

Where do you *stand* in your understanding?

Your understanding of the situation now on our precious planet?

We are shifting to a new paradigm of being.

Are you in fear or do you have greater insight and wisdom into what is unfolding?

Are you choosing the *high road* in your thinking, feeling and being?

On my fridge, for many years, I have had the saying, *"Do not follow where the path may lead. Go instead where there is no path and leave a trail."*

This saying is my *high road!*

I have endeavoured to always listen to my intuition, be courageous, be an independent thinker and not follow the mass conditioned thinking and rules – which at times leads to control, lack of personal sovereignty and less freedom.

This control has happened repeatedly throughout the centuries.

There are many other quotes referring to choosing the high road as follows:

"It is better to walk alone (in the right direction) than with a crowd going in the wrong direction." Herman Su

"It is indeed better to walk alone in the right direction than to fearfully follow the herd as they head towards the cliff." Stand in the Park Warriors

"Stand up for what you believe in, even if it means standing alone." Novak Djokovic

We ultimately have free will and free choice. So, no matter what we choose in the decisions we make – and depending on our circumstances – we first need to do our own research. This can be done through listening carefully to our own knowing and gut feeling, reading a wide range of intelligent literature and speaking with those whose views we respect. We can then be at peace with where we *stand*.

This will be our destiny or karmic path; what we are scripted to follow or create for ourself through our choices. We need to live our truth.

Remember, we are here as divine spiritual energy having a human experience and contributing to the collective wisdom of consciousness. So, wherever we stand is valid for us.

We will do well to relax, be kind and loving – especially to ourselves.

EIGHTY

The Energy of Love and Peace

This book is nearing its end, and I have thought how my perceptions have clarified during the past months. I trust you do the same. This is further to my questions in Chapter 78.

This year has shown me not to succumb to conformity of thought, and group think is not advisable.

I recently listened to a Boyer Lecture, on the radio, with the admirable Professor Michelle Simmons.[22] She is a Quantum Physicist and was Australian of the Year in 2018. Her words of advice are powerful and resonated well for me.

She advised us to:

- Admit uncertainty – we don't know everything.
- Query everything.
- Be curious.
- Doubt.
- Have self-responsibility.
- Find our truth.

A JOURNEY OF THOUGHTS

We all have infinite potential and possibilities for each hour, each day, each year to be the best it can be with the choices we make. We create our own circumstances depending on how we view ourselves.

We all have soul lessons to learn through our choices and experiences.

There is so much pain, grief, stress, hatred, anger and sorrow in the world. *Why?*

We need to hold the light, keep an open heart, and have kind thoughts and actions.

The energy of love and peace is what is needed everywhere.

Hopefully sharing my thoughts with you in this book may somehow bring more love to your heart and the way you live your life.

With love from my heart to yours.

APPENDIX

Snippets from conversations with my dear mother Elsie McKenzie since her return to spirit, aged nearly 103.

June 2017: (a month after her 'death')

"The freedom to move is wonderful (*she had been in a wheelchair for her last months*). We are malleable and can change our surroundings just by thinking.

My funeral was quite emotional for me as it was done with such dignity and joy. It was a happy end to a most happy life."

Months later:

"I see now how much you reassured me of my new existence and how I had nothing to fear in my transition into spirit."

Later again:

"I am enjoying my new freedom and actually creating new pathways for myself and finding out much about other choices I may have taken in that life with you but didn't. We always have other possibilities which would have given me other experiences.

It has been so easy for me to talk with you. So, don't forget to ask for me again soon. It is just like dialling up on the phone."

August 2018:

I asked her, "What is happening for you now Mum?"

"My world is incredible in what I am experiencing and being. The learning of great wisdom is what it is mostly about and my interaction with others is heart-warming. The wonderful wisdom and sense of peace is so inspiring and there is much magic around. I know I am losing my sense of being Elsie and my consciousness is now bringing in all my other selves who have played out other lives."

October 2018:

"You (Merriene) are liberating the core knowing of all the female members of our family tree, past, present, and future. You hold the key and have unlocked the door into greater possibilities and potential for what can be achieved.

We do not have bodies, only shapes and images of energy."

April 2019:

"My time has been most interesting with me gaining more understanding of the nature of everything and the fact energy is powerful, and our thoughts are powerful indicators of our wisdom. I am also adjusting to the new, the different and the creative force of great love and purity of action here.

The purity of intention is wonderful, and I feel light and transparent – like a spider web or fairy floss. It is so wonderful to have the ability to float through images and enjoy. You know this and know the physical world is an illusion of experiences to bring wisdom.

Know we are all progressing well here in our different endeavours. All is beautiful and nurturing."

June 2019:

"I am now in greater training to enlighten me further into the nature of reality – or a reality of sorts – as everything is an illusion apart from thought and feeling. It is so interesting to visualise a scenario and then act it out to see what the best outcome will be. We realise how asleep many of humanity are in how they live their lives and are so much in their ego state most of the time with no understanding of the big picture."

June 2020:

"I am now going into my own knowing and pulling out old memories of past learning so I can apply it now to work with many soul energies – to prepare them for their next incarnation, so to speak. It was amazing how easily these memories came back to me after that part of amnesia I had in that life with you as your mother. You see, it was all a set up so we could learn from each other – tolerance, patience – and also differences of perception."

June 25th, 2022:

(*This was my mother's birthday*)

From me: "Happy Birthday dear Mum"

"Hello dear Joan, as I called you and thank you for reaching out to me today on what would have been my birthday, and as it was my son Graham's birthday yesterday and your son Jamie's birthday the day before that."

Me: "Yes – three birthdays in three days."

"In the intervening months and years since my return to a non-physical state I have merged more with energies of a higher level and become like an eye of knowing. By this I mean I have shed my concerns I had as Elsie and exist more in a state of exploration of becomingness. Becoming a more exemplary soul with much to give in the way of deep knowing for many who are preparing for another life in the physical world – offering them choices of circumstances where they can advance to a higher state of being as they go through their adventure of being human.

And by the way, I do give you permission to use our transcriptions, our conversations between us since I returned here, in your book. You can use what you like if it can be of assistance for the reader to come to the understanding our reality beyond the physical is part of beingness. Existence does not begin or end in the physical world or when we depart it.

I can see there are many challenges facing you all and it is so important for you to take good care of all aspects of you – physical, mental, emotional, and spiritual. You are all being tested to see what your moral compass is – and many people are falling short in this regard.

So, dear daughter of mine in that life, I encourage you to rest well, nurture yourself and know you will soon emerge into a stronger, more contented you. Each day will continue to bring you new challenges but also new joys. Be grateful for the serenity your home provides for you and the lovely friendships you have with your family and select wise friends.

So many old friends of some people have not yet woken to the truth. However, this is their experience to be investigated and for them to discover what is real in their own way and time. Bless them for their position of knowing and reinforce your own knowing so you can be of help where needed.

I will leave you now with much gladness in my energy for your reaching out to me on what was my special day. Thank you for giving me much happiness during our time together. We were meant to be as we were in our relationship. All is well. Much love to you my dear.

Your dear Mum xx"

END NOTES

1. Zukav, Gary. "Soul Stories," Simon and Schuster. USA, 2007
2. Masaru Emoto. "The Hidden Messages in Water," Atria Books. USA, 2005
3. Kondo, Marie, "The Life-Changing Magic of Tidying," Vermillion Mass Market, USA 2014
4. Arrowsmith-Young, Barbara. "The Woman Who Changed Her Brain," HarperCollins. USA. 2012
5. Manguel, Alberto. "Curiosity," Yale University Press. USA. 2016
6. Emery, Adrian. "Personal Sovereignty," NSW, Australia. 2019 https://www.adrianemery.com/
7. Farrés, Osvaldo and Joe Davis, "Perhaps, Perhaps, Perhaps," Sung by Doris Day, from the Album "Latin for Lovers." 1964
8. Weir, Alison. "Mary Boleyn," Vintage Arrow Mass Market, UK. 2012
9. Reader's Digest Editors. 'Reader's Digest Word Power Dictionary,' Reader's Digest. USA. 2001
10. Marciniak, Barbara. "Path of Empowerment," New World Library. USA. 2004.
11. Tucker, Linda. "Mystery of the White Lions," Hay House. USA. 2010
12. Skiff, Jennifer. https://jenniferskiff.com/
13. Meyerhoff Hieronimus, J. Zohara. "White Spirit Animals: Prophets of Change," Bear & Company. USA. 2017
14. Skiff, Jennifer. "Rescuing Ladybugs," New World Library. USA. 2018
15. The song is a classic English language nursery rhyme dating back to 1852. https://en.wikipedia.org/wiki/Row,_Row,_Row_Your_Boat
16. Marciniak, Barbara. "Path of Empowerment," New World Library. USA. 2004.

17 Fox Searchlight Productions. "A United Kingdom," UK. 2016 https://www.imdb.com/title/tt3387266/
18 Morrison, Zoe. "Music and Freedom," Random House Australia. Aust. 2016
19 'Know Thyself' is a timeless philosophical inscription carved into stone over the entrance to the Temple of Apollo in the ancient Greek precinct of Delphi.
20 Suzuki, David and Peter Knudtson. "The Wisdom of the Elders," Bantam Dell, USA. 1999
21 Powers, Richard. "The Overstory," Vintage Arrow. USA. 2019
22 Professor Michelle Simmons: https://cms.australianoftheyear.org.au/recipients/professor-michelle-yvonne-simmons-ao#:~:text=Since%20arriving%20in%20Australia%20from,with%20the%20world's%20thinnest%20wire.

RECOMMENDED READING

Arrowsmith-Young, Barbara. *"The Woman Who Changed Her Brain,"* HarperCollins. USA. 2012

Emery, Adrian. *"Personal Sovereignty,"* NSW, Australia. 2019 https://www.adrianemery.com/

Kondo, Marie. *"The Life-Changing Magic of Tidying,"* Vermillion Mass Market. USA 2014

Manguel, Alberto. *"Curiosity,"* Yale University Press. USA. 2016

Marciniak, Barbara. *"Path of Empowerment,"* New World Library. USA. 2004.

Masaru Emoto. *"The Hidden Messages in Water,"* Atria Books. USA, 2005

Meyerhoff Hieronimus, J. Zohara. *"White Spirit Animals: Prophets of Change,"* Bear & Company. USA. 2017

Morrison, Zoe. *"Music and Freedom,"* Random House Australia. Aust. 2016

Powers, Richard. *"The Overstory,"* Vintage Arrow. USA. 2019

Scott, Digby. *"Change Makers,"* New Zealand. 2019. https://www.digbyscott.com/

Scott, Merriene. *"The World Beyond Today,"* WA, Australia. 2001

Scott, Merriene. *"Adventure into Transformation,"* WA, Australia. 2003

Scott, Merriene. *"Ancient Memories, New Beginnings,"* WA, Australia 2004

Skiff, Jennifer. *"Rescuing Ladybugs,"* New World Library. USA. 2018

Skiff, Jennifer. *"The Divinity of Dogs,"* Hay House. USA. 2012

Suzuki, David and Peter Knudtson. *"The Wisdom of the Elders,"* Bantam Dell, USA. 1999

Tucker, Linda. *"Mystery of the White Lions,"* Hay House. USA. 2010

Weir, Alison. *"Mary Boleyn,"* Vintage Arrow Mass Market, UK. 2012

Zukav, Gary. *"Soul Stories,"* Simon and Schuster. USA, 2007

FEEDBACK FROM READERS AND CLIENTS

"I always enjoy your newsletters; they so much express what I too am feeling, and I like your new book and reading your wise words. The book should have 365 chapters for the entire year."

(From a friend Peter Krusi in Zurich, Switzerland)

"I have total admiration for you. The writing in your 'curiosity' piece is so good. After all, it's not as though you did a 'writing course' or whatever. On top of that, it's just what I needed after a somewhat difficult day today."

(From a friend in Oregon, USA)

"I agree with your newsletter – such a gorgeous hymn to remind us of the beauty around us." (I wrote about the hymn 'All Things Bright and Beautiful')

"That's a great newsletter! Perfect timing for Spring. And I love that the chemist staff at the Pharmacy put your newsletters up in their staff room."

"Thank you for your contribution to the wellbeing of all living forms and the magic of our planet."

"I keep your books close to me, often reading a paragraph or two each morning. Thank you for sharing your gift of divined wisdom. You are a wonderful human being."

   (From acclaimed author Jennifer Skiff, Perth, and USA.)

"Merriene remains a humble person. I respect the wisdom of the awakened consciousness revealed in her books. I believe Merriene offers blessings to all people with whom she interacts."

"I was sent your second book 'Adventure into Transformation' for my birthday, and I loved it so much that I am ordering it for another friend for her birthday and I am ordering the third book for myself. The ideas are not new to me, but I love the way you present them and have enjoyed making your book part of my morning meditation/alignment practice. Thank you for shining a little more light into my days."

   (From a reader in North Carolina, USA)

"I feel specially blessed to have met you and to feel the beauty of your spirit and soul. You have been chosen by God to care for people in need, taking them to worlds beyond, where they might never go otherwise. You give us love and courage to be our true selves – bringing solace thereby. You relate to the invisible realms more readily than the visible. You make sense of the inexplicable, unknown, imaginary world of wonder, and make them simple to understand."

   (From a wonderful client)

"I took the book you gave me ('Ancient Memories, New Beginnings') to the waiting room at the eye checkup this afternoon and was enchanted by the solid but simple language and the Light that shone off the pages into my heart."

(From acclaimed author of the book *'God's Call Girl'* Carla van Raay)

ABOUT THE AUTHOR

Merriene Scott is an author, educator, intuitive clairvoyant and gifted automatic writer. Well-known in her hometown of Perth, Western Australia, Merriene is the author of the inspirational book trilogy, "Messages from Illanitis," and monthly newsletter, which she publishes to her growing local and international audience. Originally trained as a teacher, Merriene married a farmer and then later, with her husband, bought and ran a General Store in a tourist town by the ocean in the beautiful south west of Western Australia.

On separating from her husband, Merriene embarked on a career in counselling and writing. In this role she has helped clients from across the world - some who she has never met in the physical world – including England, USA, Central Africa, and Central Australia. She even assisted a next-door neighbour who would give her questions, as she being a clairvoyant counsellor, was too busy with her own clients!

Her work also includes guiding clients of all ages - ranging from teens through to people in their eighties - to discover more about themselves, their purpose, choices and to get in touch with loved ones who have died. It is mostly a sacred and comforting experience for both her clients and herself.

This book is written mainly through intuitive knowing, not automatic writing, and offers Merriene's thoughts during the changing seasons and events in her life via monthly newsletters. Hence the variation in levels of thought put forward.

Her two wonderful and successful sons and three lovely grandchildren bring her much delight and interest in their colourful lives. Merriene lives in Perth, Western Australia, near the stunningly blue Indian Ocean, where she regularly swims and walks in nature's beauty.

Contact Merriene Scott

Merriene welcomes your feedback and queries. Please contact her at:

merriene@merrienescott.com
www.merrienescott.com

www.ingramcontent.com/pod-product-compliance
Lightning Source LLC
Chambersburg PA
CBHW051944290426
44110CB00015B/2098